A Publication of the
National Center for Nonprofit Boards

The Board Member's Guide to Fund Raising: What Every Trustee Needs to Know About Raising Money by Fisher Howe represents a project of the National Center for Nonprofit Boards (NCNB) and Jossey-Bass Publishers. The mission of the NCNB is to improve the effectiveness of nonprofit organizations by strengthening their boards of directors. NCNB offers three programs and services to meet the governance needs of the nonprofit community:

1. The *Board Development Consultation Service* helps nonprofits design and conduct board development workshops and retreats tailored to their board members and chief executives, and provides speakers for conferences and meetings.
2. The *Information Center* is a nationwide service that responds to written and telephone inquiries on a broad range of topics affecting nonprofit boards.
3. The *Publication Program* offers booklets, texts, and audiotapes on key issues in nonprofit governance.

The National Center for Nonprofit Boards was established in 1988 by the Association of Governing Boards of Universities and Colleges and INDEPENDENT SECTOR. Initial funding for the Center was provided by the W. K. Kellogg Foundation, Beatrice Foundation, Exxon Fund for Management Assistance of the New York Community Trust, William and Flora Hewlett Foundation, Lilly Endowment, Mobil Foundation, Rockefeller Brothers Fund, and the Warner-Lambert Foundation.
For more information about the Center's publications, Board Development Consultation Service, or Information Center, or to be added to NCNB's mailing list, please contact:

National Center for Nonprofit Boards
Suite 411
2000 L Street, N.W.
Washington, D.C. 20036
Tel: 202-452-6262
Fax: 202-452-6299

The Board Member's Guide to Fund Raising

Fisher Howe

The Board Member's Guide to Fund Raising

*What Every Trustee
Needs to Know
About Raising Money*

Jossey-Bass Publishers · San Francisco

THE BOARD MEMBER'S GUIDE TO FUND RAISING
What Every Trustee Needs to Know About Raising Money
  by Fisher Howe

Copyright © 1991 by: Jossey-Bass Inc., Publishers
                     350 Sansome Street
                     San Francisco, California 94104

Library of Congress Cataloging-in-Publication Data

Howe, Fisher, date.
    The board member's guide to fund raising : what every trustee
needs to know about raising money / Fisher Howe.
        p.   cm.—(Jossey-Bass nonprofit sector series)
    Includes bibliographical references and index.
    ISBN 1-55542-322-1
    1. Fund raising—United States.   2. Corporations, Nonprofit—
United States.   3. Directors of corporations—United States.
I. Title.   II. Series.
HV41.9.U5H68   1991
658.15'224—dc20   90-23533
                                                            CIP

Manufactured in the United States of America

The paper used in this book meets the State of California
requirements for recycled paper (50 percent recycled waste,
including 10 percent post-consumer waste), which are the strictest
guidelines for recycled paper currently in use in
the United States.

JACKET DESIGN BY WILLI BAUM

FIRST EDITION
  HB Printing   10 9 8 7 6 5 4 3

Code 9122

The Jossey-Bass
Nonprofit Sector Series

Contents

Foreword

Many years ago, near the end of the last century, my grandfather, John D. Rockefeller, made a statement about fund raising that has often served as a guide for my own philanthropic activities. It was a simple rule: "Never think you need to apologize for asking someone to give to a worthy object."

With this book Fisher Howe has picked up where my grandfather left off. He not only provides encouragement to those responsible for raising funds for not-for-profit organizations but also supplies useful suggestions on how to approach this daunting task.

I am happy to say he is fully qualified to undertake this job, which is especially necessary at a time when competition for the philanthropic dollar has never been more intense. Fisher Howe served with distinction in our foreign service and as a member of the State Department's Policy Planning Council. For many years, he was a dean of the Johns Hopkins University's School of Advanced International Studies. Most recently, he acted as a consultant to a number of not-for-profit organizations. Mr. Howe has, quite literally, put into practice what he writes about in this stimulating book.

It comes as no surprise that these are difficult times for the philanthropic world, but they are also times of enormous opportunity. In large measure the not-for-profits have been asked to take on some of the toughest challenges we face in sustaining both our global society and our individual communities. To be effective in their tasks they must rely on strong, dedicated, and courageous boards of trustees. These boards must be informed and fearless in seeking financial help to carry out their work.

Fisher Howe's research on this subject has unearthed some astonishing facts. At the present time there are between 600,000 and 1.5 million not-for-profit institutions of all kinds in the United States. These organizations are dedicated to service in the widest array of activities, including, but by no means limited to, medical research, the environment, religion, education, health care, drug rehabilitation, the homeless, disaster relief, and the arts; each organization has a governing board of anywhere from 10 to 100 members. Doing some rough arithmetic makes it abundantly clear that there are at least 20 million of our fellow citizens serving as trustees who must, by agreeing to serve, take on some responsibility for raising money.

Although there are innumerable books filled with fundraising materials that teach the latest techniques for proposal writing, the use of "direct mail," or the best way to approach foundations and corporations, what has been missing until now is a sense of how the individual trustee can best use his or her own special talents as an integral—indeed vital—part of the support process.

Fisher Howe has now filled this void.

December 1990   David Rockefeller

Preface

Charitable and other nonprofit organizations, by definition, live by donations from their supporters. Where businesses rely on sales and governments depend on appropriations, nonprofit organizations, such as schools, colleges, churches, hospitals, welfare agencies, museums, theaters, advocacy groups, and professional associations, are sustained in large part by voluntary contributions. Although many such organizations derive an important part of their income from revenue-producing programs, all but a few that maintain commercially successful enterprises must continue to rely on contributed funds to sustain their main programs. For most organizations, ticket sales, tuition, gift shops, and health care insurance reimbursements, however imaginatively managed, do not cover all the costs of providing performers, teachers, other professionals, or administrative staff. Services provided by nonprofit organizations are thus made possible mainly by contributions that result from active fund raising.

It is ironic and unfortunate, therefore, that the very people most closely associated with nonprofit institutions—the board members—are so often heard to say, "I'll do anything but raise money!"

Often the denial of fund-raising responsibility is put in these terms:

- "Ours is a working board; we deal with substantive programs, not with the raising of money."
- "They promised me I would not have to do fund raising."

Board members who believe that fund raising is not part of their responsibility simply need to be disabused of the notion.

But you also hear the reluctance expressed in these different ways:

- "I won't prey on my friends."
- "I can't stand being turned down."
- "I can't sell; I am just not good at it."
- "I bring other expertise to the organization."
- "I have a conflict; I'm raising money for others."
- "I said I would just lend my name."
- "I'm too busy."

Behind these comments are many explanations. For some people, asking for money is simply distasteful; they see it as begging or pressuring friends. Others in all sincerity believe that they are just not cut out for fund raising. Some are genuinely fearful: They find it scary just to think about asking for money. Some can't stand the thought of being turned down. Particularly unhelpful are those who serve on a board only for the prestige it brings them. You can even hear those who suggest, "With all those fund raisers out there, why don't we just hire a good one to raise the money for us?"

If a nonprofit organization is to be successful, it must recognize these common attitudes and deal with them forthrightly. The first step is to have the members of the board understand fully the problems and challenges involved in fund raising. In particular, trustees must be clear about their own role as board members.

Private philanthropy has come to be known as the "third sector," to differentiate it from government and business. In the United States today there are estimated to be 1.25 million nonprofit, voluntary, charitable, and religious organizations. Their operating budgets add up to over $2 billion. As a major share of those budgets is supported by *contributed* dollars, it is essential that the responsibility for raising the money be clear and the management of fund-raising activities be effective; otherwise, organizations simply cannot exist.

Thus the fund-raising world is big and it is competitive. It is big in the sense that the potential for support is as wide as the number of people who can be reached by mail and as high as the largest gift of the most generous donor. It is competitive in the sense that nonprofit organizations in every field are seeking the same philanthropic dollar. The message is clear: To survive and flourish, an organization must be thorough, orderly, and deliberate in its fund-raising program.

The variety of institutions within the third sector is extraordinary: tax-exempt, voluntary, and philanthropic organizations such as schools, hospitals, libraries, social services, and those for recreation and housing; civic, social, and fraternal organizations; arts and cultural organizations; foundations; and religious institutions such as churches, synagogues, and mosques, with their affiliated schools and community services. Each institution within each type has its own individuality: It is large or small, young or old, strong or weak. Each organization has its own environment, its own constituency, its own needs.

Each therefore must deal with its fund raising in its own way. Yet success is likely to attend some fund-raising methods and failure is almost certain with others. How the trustees deal with their fund-raising responsibility and any reluctance among its members, therefore, is vital to the organization's welfare, indeed to its survival.

Board members are as varied as the organizations they serve. Some, new to trusteeship, are naive, eager, and wrapped up in the program of the institution. Others—prominent, successful men and women—are accustomed to board deliberations, confident in their knowledge of how nonprofit organizations work. Some board members are well versed in fund-raising matters; others are untutored and probably unhappy in raising funds to support the programs. Although they all must concern themselves with fund raising, they bring a variety of both experience and attitude to the responsibility. These chapters seek to embrace this range from innocence to sophistication, from open receptiveness to reluctance and distaste for fund raising. The requisite for making good use of the book is a desire to help the nonprofit organization to which a commitment of leadership has been made.

As a trustee, then, just what should you know and what should you do about fund raising? One certainty shines through: Fund raising is not learned from a book. As with skiing, dancing, or playing golf, you can get a sense of how to go about fund raising from reading and watching, but you learn by doing. Accordingly, this is not a "how-to" book. Instead of offering answers and solutions, it seeks to present a helpful way of looking at fund raising so that the job, being better understood, will get done.

The book explains the principles of fund raising from the board member perspective, offering some do's and don'ts in the successful implementation of those principles. In effect, each section and chapter could open with the salutation:

> Dear Board Member: You will have to reach decisions appropriate to your own organization, but on *this* aspect of fund raising, *this* is the problem and *this* is what you should know about it. . . ." (By inference, "this other" is what you don't need to bother yourself with.)

The selection of topics has been governed by two factors: (1) the fund-raising questions most frequently asked about in seminars, workshops, and board briefings; and (2) where boards most frequently go wrong, as revealed in professional audits and feasibility studies.

One question constantly arises: In fund raising, what is the role of trustees and what is the role of the staff? Although in the final analysis responsibility for the success or failure of fund raising lies with the board, it is quite clear that the board is helpless without the staff—the executive and development office. But no categorical delineation can be made of the part each will play. Every organization will be different, again depending on size, history of fund raising, and the personalities of the board and staff members. In some the staff does virtually all the money raising; in others the trustees play the dominant role.

Because the chief executive and development staff have indispensable parts of the action, including helping the board members to be effective in their roles, they must be looking over the shoulder as board members read this book. Wherever possible, the place of trustees in relation to executive and staff is identified, but don't look for definitive answers; each organization must develop its own pattern. Regardless of what part the staff plays, however, trustees must oversee, evaluate performance, and participate. They cannot run away from fund raising.

Some will say there is nothing to fund raising but common sense, hard work, and an abiding enthusiasm for the institution you want to help. Others assert that fund raising calls for highly specialized techniques and therefore for professional expertise. Reality, as usual, is somewhere in between.

Because the board of trustees is the central focus of this book, the presentation starts and ends with board *leadership*: what the board's responsibility is (Chapter One) and how the board and its members can be effective in fulfilling this responsibility (Chapter Nine).

Between the opening and concluding chapters, the book looks at key elements of a successful fund-raising program, particularly as board members should understand and participate in them.

- *Concepts* that relate to the mission, case, and constituency are fundamental to the fund raising of all organizations and should be understood by trustees (Chapter Two).
- Differing techniques and procedures need to be understood in seeking support from each of the several *sources of support*— individuals (Chapter Three); government agencies, foundations, business, and other nonprofit organizations (Chapter Four).
- *Raising capital funds* presents a different array of problems for

which board members have a special responsibility (Chapter
Five).

- Trustees can be of great help in specific *support activities,* such
as publicity, cultivation of prospects, and research and preparation (Chapter Six).
- The board's challenge in fund raising comes in the actual *asking.* The hurdles are discussed and a scenario is offered in Chapter Six.
- The board has an oversight responsibility to assure the effectiveness of the fund-raising *organization and procedures,* notably in
regard to development staff, volunteers and training, procedures
and computers, strategy, and costs (Chapter Seven).
- *Special concerns,* such as cause-related marketing, ethical matters, and the use of consultants, often involve the board (Chapter
Eight).

Returning to *leadership,* Chapter Nine looks at the ways a
board can usefully deal with its own composition, organization,
and motivation of members and can assure its own continued
effectiveness.

The reader may choose to read *The Board Member's Guide to Fund
Raising* straight through to get an overview of key fund-raising
issues, strategies, and methods. It was designed to be read by a busy
trustee in the time it takes to fly from LaGuardia to O'Hare. On the
other hand, the reader may prefer to skip to subjects of current
interest. Both board members and staff can keep a copy on hand as
a resource, ready when a new fund-raising subject arises. Capital
campaigns, cause-related marketing, or hiring new development
staff, although perhaps not of present interest, may become so in a
few months.

One caveat must be stressed: Where legal implications are
involved, this book cannot be a substitute for legal counsel.

The discussion, I hope, carries another message. Through a better
understanding of what is involved in fund raising, board members
of all shapes and sizes, young and old, naive and worldly, may find
that asking for support for their organizations need not be as oner-

ous and forbidding as they had thought. Indeed, they can come to realize that contributing to the success of a worthy institution by strengthening its funding base can bring a world of satisfaction.

I owe an enormous debt to my brother, David L. Howe, of Charlotte, North Carolina, former schoolmaster and wordsmith *extraordinaire*. With gentle ruthlessness he worked tirelessly over many drafts. He has the knack of giving a sentence twice the strength in half the words. He did throughout.

I am also greatly indebted to my partner, David G. Lavender, of Ojai, California, who has generously and wisely led me into and around the tortuous paths of management and fund-raising consultancy.

Washington, D.C.   Fisher Howe
December 1990

For D. F. H.

The Author

Fisher Howe, a former foreign service officer and a graduate of Harvard, is a consultant for nonprofit organizations with the firm of Lavender/Howe & Associates, which has offices in Ojai, California, and Washington, D.C. His previous management and fundraising experience includes positions of assistant dean and executive director at the Johns Hopkins University School of Advanced International Studies; and director of institutional relations, Resources for the Future, a research organization in Washington, D.C. for energy, natural resources, and the environment.

Howe has been a trustee of several organizations, including Fountain Valley School in Colorado Springs, Hospice of D.C., Washington Area Council on Alcohol and Drug Abuse, Metropolitan Washington United Way, St. John's Child Development Center, Bureau of Rehabilitation (offender half-way houses), Pilgrim Society (Plymouth, Massachusetts), and the Washington chapter of the National Society of Fund Raising Executives.

His publications include "What You Need to Know About Fund Raising," *Harvard Business Review,* and "Fund Raising and the Nonprofit Board Member," National Center for Nonprofit Boards.

The Board Member's Guide to Fund Raising

1

The Board Member's Perspective:
How a Board Member
Should Look at Fund Raising

1. The Board's Responsibility
2. Giving and Asking

1. The Board's Responsibility

Start with the first principle: The board of a nonprofit organization is responsible for governing the organization and ensuring that it succeeds in its mission. That responsibility—no matter what the size of the organization or the nature of its mission—includes seeing that the organization has the resources required to carry out that mission. The board must establish the organization and procedures to get the fund-raising job done. In turn, board members must be involved, individually and personally. If an institution is having trouble raising money, don't look to the development office; don't look to the chief executive; first check out the board of trustees.

1

One need only look at institutions around us—schools, churches, hospitals, museums, public interest groups—to be persuaded that nonprofit organizations with sound financial support have strong trustee membership and knowledgeable people committed to and actively involved with the institution. The converse is more impressive: Nonprofit organizations that have trouble raising funds have boards with indifferent members who are either distracted by other commitments or unwilling to face up to their full responsibility. Strong boards mean strong finances while weak finances point to weakness in the board. Trustees cannot close their eyes to their responsibility or pass it off onto others.

This role of the board to ensure adequate resources must be viewed in the context of the board's total responsibility. In essence, the charge to a nonprofit board has three components: *fiduciary, programmatic,* and *financial.*

Fiduciary involves protecting the public interest. In this respect, the board must fulfill the legal requirements, such as incorporation and framing the by-laws; maintain the integrity of the institution through audits and avoidance of conflicts of interest; select, pay, evaluate, and if necessary dismiss the chief executive; and ensure its own leadership effectiveness by responsibly selecting members and officers and by establishing constructive board procedures.

Programmatic means to satisfy the needs and expectations of the constituent community in fulfilling its mission. That is, the board must define the organization's mission and purposes; what it is to do and (often neglected) what it is not to do; see to the plans— for the short and long run—and the setting of priorities; approve policies and major commitments through involvement in the budget process; and ensure periodic evaluation of program performance.

Financial means to assure the viability of the organization. Here, the board must see that adequate funding resources are obtained to sustain the organization and its program and oversee the financial operations through appropriate budgetary, investment, and accounting procedures.

Board members may take particular interest in, and make their greatest contribution to, one or another of these responsibilities. But every member must recognize all of them and realize that fund raising is often the most vital and inescapable. The buck starts and stops with the board. Members must be fully involved.

It is relevant to emphasize that the responsibilities of a board of a *nonprofit* organization differ from those of a board of a *for-profit*, commercial company. This difference is frequently overlooked or mistaken. Raise a caution flag when you hear such statements as

- "What we need to do is bring some business efficiency to this charity organization." (The exact nature of this "business efficiency" is left undefined.)
- "Nonprofit organizations need to be more businesslike." ("Businesslike" can mean a lot of things, or nothing. If you mean "carefully arranged, well carried out," well and good; if you mean "run like a commercial enterprise," beware.)
- "When you come down to it, a good company board member is bound to be just as effective on a nonprofit board." (Simply not so. Of course, many corporate leaders make first-class nonprofit trustees, but many do not. The roles are quite different.)

Because the subject relates quite directly to fund raising, the differences between the for-profit and the not-for-profit worlds are worth further exploration.*

One authority put it this way (Conrad, 1986, p. 1): "There is no question that nonprofits can be better managed and we need to understand more about what better nonprofit management means. However, better management does not equal more 'businesslike.' There are universal management concepts, but they are not the sole property of business. But what makes a business a business is not the same as what makes a nonprofit a nonprofit."

Nonprofit organizations exist for public service; they live by donations and they answer to the general public they serve. Companies, on the other hand, are in business to make money; they live

*This discussion throughout is concerned with nonprofit organizations that have received tax-exempt status under the Internal Revenue Service Code 501(c)(3); it does not deal with political fund raising, an altogether different activity.

by sales and profits; they answer to their stockholders. Remember that chief executive Alfred Sloan said, "GM doesn't make cars, it makes money." These underlying differences are reflected in how they are governed.

Other differences include constituencies and make-up of the boards. The constituency of a nonprofit organization is twofold: those who benefit and those who support it. The constituency of a commercial corporation is the customer, the purchaser of products or services; the owners and stockholders are the beneficiaries. Budgets of nonprofit organizations are designed to assure satisfactory services and to keep institutions alive; budgets for companies assure profits. Corporations have boards of directors who are paid handsomely for their efforts; nonprofit organizations have boards of trustees who are unpaid volunteers.

Of course both nonprofit organizations and commercial corporations need to minimize costs, design and promote goods and services to meet user needs, and manage personnel and resources effectively. Both benefit from competition—commerce more than charity. With good reason, people in business look to the "bottom line," quite literally the bottom right column figure showing success or failure. If there is a bottom line in a nonprofit organization, it is its effectiveness in public service performance, or in increasing knowledge as in a research institution—products that are not readily measurable. Though good "corporate citizenship," a company doing its share in the community, is altogether worthy—corporate giving does have a philanthropic dimension—it is predicated on self-interest, happily being also favorable to the public weal.

A significant difference between nonprofit and corporate boards, one that directly relates to fund raising, is in the customary board size and composition. Corporate boards tend to be small and efficient, with members selected for what they can contribute to the profit-making potential. Boards of trustees of charitable organizations, on the other hand, are generally large in order to enlist the many skills a board needs, to reach a wide spectrum of the community, and to get widespread personal involvement in the fund-raising effort.

In sum, tax-exempt institutions deal with different fiduciary, programmatic, and financial constraints that lead directly to different personnel motivations (in business, people are employed; they don't volunteer) and to different bases for evaluating performance. Nowhere do these differences appear more starkly than in the fund-raising responsibilities of a nonprofit organization's board of trustees.

Boards of trustees of nonprofit organizations, even as boards of directors of commercial businesses, must stay clear of encroaching on management responsibilities. For trustees, however, the fund-raising responsibility calls for more direct personal involvement and participation in the operations than in any of its other responsibilities. In itself important, this also represents a significant difference from corporate boards of directors.

Board and Staff Division of Labor

Although the trustees' overall responsibility for fund raising is clear, determining who does the work is another matter. A board is generally quite helpless without the chief executive and, in a large organization, the professional fund-raising staff, usually called the development or advancement office. The division of labor among board, chief executive, and development staff is an important consideration for every organization.

Depending on the size, the nature of the mission, and the personalities involved, organizations will determine who will handle the various fund-raising functions. As the discussion of the manifold elements of a fund-raising program will show, some organizations will look to the executive officer to make most of the solicitations, occasionally calling on trustees to assist. Other organizations, often community service institutions with less extensive staff, will rely heavily on board members to do the asking for donations—from individuals, companies, and foundations. For both large and small organizations, however, the major burdens of planning, research, preparation, drafting proposals, and particularly of taking initiative must fall on the executive and his staff.

As the board is ultimately responsible, it must oversee the fund-raising effort; trustees skirt this role at their peril. In addition, discussion of the various aspects of fund raising shows that trustees can be positively helpful in many ways. In some activities, such as capital campaigns, or in some circumstances, such as cause-related marketing, the board must get closely involved.

Boards usually find it helpful to have a development committee to bring focus and force to its own efforts and to work most closely with the development staff (see Section Twenty-Four). Development committees can indeed be helpful in motivating fellow board members, in planning and assigning tasks, and in generally overseeing the fund-raising activities of the chief executive and staff. Boards, however, must guard against complacent withdrawal, believing they have turned over to the committee their responsibility for raising money.

Finally, some boards have found it useful to create an auxiliary body—a "foundation," a "corporate council"—to handle some or all of the fund-raising tasks. Such a device has its attraction; in some instances it can be positively helpful. But again, beware the delusion that the board can turn over its responsibility to others. The board can enlist assistance, but it must not be seduced into thinking it can say someone else is responsible for assuring that adequate funds are raised for the organization.

2. Giving and Asking

Although giving money and asking for support are everyday processes, they are frequently misunderstood. This misunderstanding, even on the part of leaders in the philanthropic world, gives rise to much of the distaste and avoidance associated with fund raising. To understand at the outset what is involved is crucial to fund-raising success.

Some pervasive principles—basic truths—of why people give underlie all charitable giving. They must be recognized if fund raising is to be successful. They apply across the full span of philanthropic contributions: donations from individuals, foundations, and corporations; even grants made by one nonprofit organization to another, such as a church or community service club making a grant to an arts or charitable institution.

Here are six principles of philanthropic giving:

1. *People give money because they want to.* Making a contribution to an organization of one's choice in almost every case

gives satisfaction, even pleasure, to the donor. It is neither distasteful nor an unwanted burden. Asking for money, therefore, is not an act of arm-twisting; you are not trying to force someone to do something they don't want to do.

Think of your own giving: If you give to your church, your alma mater, and your own favorite charities, you do so because you want to. You are solicited, in person or by mail, but you give of your own accord. You can say "No." Even when you choose to decline, you don't hold it against the people who have asked you to give unless they are overbearing, tactless, or unfriendly in their request or toward your response.

2. *People don't give unless they are asked.* With few exceptions, contributions are made in response to a request; they rarely come in out of the blue. Certainly no organization can count on windfalls; simply being known and approved does not cause money to flow in: You must ask.

An important corollary: *People do not make large donations unless they are asked to consider large donations.* Prospective contributors are not resentful of being asked to consider a major gift; indeed, they may be flattered. They may not give the amount suggested, but their ultimate contribution will almost surely be greater for having been asked to give the larger amount.

3. *People give money to people.* This is no less true for being a cliché. The personal equation in giving and asking is all important—person-to-person relationships underlie philanthropy. They play a key part not only in contributions from individuals, but also in the seemingly less personal corporate, foundation, and government grants.

Though a prospective donor must of course be interested in an organization and what it does, it is the people involved—who it is that asks for the gift—that count toward the actual donation. Even in mail solicitations, you look to see who signs, who is on the letterhead, who are the friends or distinguished people asking for your annual contribution.

If the personal element is so important, what is it that matters most in the asker? Not necessarily prominence, familiarity, or congeniality. The one quality more than all others a contributor looks for in the person asking is *respect:* Does the prospect respect

the asker? Again, look to your own experience: When you are solicited in person or by mail, you look to see who is asking and, even
subconsciously, you let your judgment of that person guide you.
You respond accordingly.

4. *People give money to opportunities, not to needs.* The
chance to help an institution achieve an aspiration, meet a challenge, is more appealing than to help it make up a shortage or to
bail it out. Although an organization must know its own funding
needs—precisely what the money is being raised to do—when it
goes out to raise the money, it should emphasize what the money
will accomplish. It should speak of deeds, not needs.

5. In the same vein, *people give to success, not to distress.*
Even as you ask others to help you fulfill opportunities rather than
cover your current needs, so the request for support must show
achievement, not despair. Be clear on what is involved here. Your
organization may be raising funds to deal with the distress of others—hunger, sickness, a natural disaster; it must avoid asking for
support because of its own distress. It is mighty difficult to raise
money to cover a deficit. Everyone wants to help someone who is
doing something positive, is achieving. Everyone likes a winner.

6. Finally and most important: *People give money to make
a change for the good.* Small contributions and large donations are
made with varied reasons and motivations—public recognition, as-
suaging guilt, gratitude, personal gain—but, far more than for any
other reason, people give because an organization is doing something worthwhile, is making a change for the good in other people's
lives.

Of course there are exceptions to these principles. Sometimes
contributions seem to be determined by a high-level give and take:
One corporate leader or prominent citizen gives in return for someone's donation to another organization. Although such giving ex-
changes do take place, they do not reflect the motivation for the
majority of ongoing charitable giving.

Whether a donation is to be $5 or $5 million, a donor wants
to see the money go to an institution seeking to help, to make a
change, to make something better, to fill a community need. Institutions asking for money must constantly put themselves in the
contributor's position and show what it is they are doing that helps

the community meet some problem in a way that can make the world better, happier, or more livable.

If these six principles say something about the giving side of the equation, what about the asking side?

A number of axioms flow from why people give; others turn out to be simply the characteristics of successful asking.

- Ego is deeply involved in all giving; ego must be respected and even played upon by the asker.
- Because people tend to give emotionally rather than rationally, they need to be offered hopes and visions.
- Though the impulse to give is usually spontaneous, sometimes instantaneous, the actual decision to make a gift is rarely made on a first asking.
- Few first gifts are major; wise askers gratefully nurture a small gift into a later big one.
- When a donor of a major gift denies interest in recognition, take care: Frequently such donors do want and deserve multiple expressions of appreciation and some public recognition. Insist that a request for anonymity be confirmed, perhaps by later asking permission of the donor to make public acknowledgment of the gift.
- Though tax advantages can be critically important to how a gift is made and, in some cases, to how large a gift will be, only in the case of planned giving and estate planning are tax advantages a central consideration. In most circumstances, askers can make tax considerations incidental, a mere footnote to the request for a gift.
- Many major donors are either on the board of the receiving institution or active participants in its programs; recruiting donor prospects into the organization is therefore central to securing future major gifts.
- It is well to assume that husbands and wives share in gift-making decisions; involve couples in both the cultivation and the asking.
- The best person to ask for a gift is not necessarily the first one to volunteer nor a close friend of the prospect. Although such people may be of great help in the approach, the best person to

do the asking is the one known to be most highly respected by
the donor.
- Children of prospects generally are not good askers; it is too easy
  for the parents to say No.

Although all the foregoing factors are important, none is as essential to success as the enthusiasm the asker brings to the activity.

So, in sum, trustees must hold two things in mind in addressing
their responsibility for raising money. First, they must recognize
and accept that asking for money is not something to be seen as
hurtful and unpleasant. They are neither pressuring nor invading
someone's personal domain when they ask for support for their
organization. It need not be an unpleasant task. Second, boards
must be ever aware of the importance of direct, interpersonal relationships in all giving and asking. This means that in any important solicitation, deliberate attention must be given to selecting who
should do the asking and how that asking should be carried out.

2

Providing a Strong Foundation
for Fund Raising:
The Underlying Elements

3. The Mission, Planning, and Assessment of Funding Needs

Too often organizations start on a fund-raising drive honestly believing they have a clear program on which everyone agrees when
in fact there are significant inconsistencies: Program directions are
confused, priorities are contradictory, or board and staff do not
agree. For a number of important reasons, but particularly as a
foundation for the fund-raising program, clarity and agreement on
mission and *long-range plans* are essential.

Mission Statement

An organization may prepare a mission statement in a single, carefully crafted paragraph as a simple description of what the orga-

11

nization does, for use in an annual report or in pamphlets and brochures. Such a limited statement, however, is not helpful for fund-raising purposes. It can actually be harmful if, through its carefully managed wording, key issues are submerged or fundamental purposes are left unstated.

A more useful mission statement, a document for *internal* use, the product of self-examination, is one that is explicit on the organization's purpose and programs. (It is not to be confused with the case statement. Although derived from the mission, a case statement is an *external* document telling prospective supporters why they would want to make a contribution.)

Strategic Planning

A structured strategic or long-range planning exercise is often the best approach to the preparation of a mission statement. The mission statement will be what comes out of a planning exercise, not what goes into it; it will be the core understanding around which can be built a clear, unambiguous articulation of purposes, programs, and priorities—clearly of great value to board and management. It also affords a firm basis for arriving at an estimate of the resources needed to support the organization on which a fund-raising program depends.

A strategic or long-range planning effort should address a wide range of fundamental questions, all of which have importance in fund raising.

- Why is the organization in business to begin with? What would the world be like without it?
- What other similar organizations are there in the community? Is there unnecessary competition? What is the organization's comparative advantage? What cooperation or division of effort is possible?
- What are the strongest and weakest features of the organization? of its programs?
- Are the priorities for effort and expenditure spelled out?
- What are the long- and short-range objectives? Can realistic

goals be set—operational markers along the way to achieving the major objectives?

• Have the funding needs—programmatic and administrative— been factored into the plans? Has an appropriate funding effort been incorporated into both planning and priorities?

Trustees should assure themselves on the *process* of planning as well. Have board, management, and program staff been involved in the planning and the mission statement? Is there a system of periodic review of forward plans and priorities?

Here is one test of the adequacy of the planning. Give a serious answer to this question: What program, facilities, and administrative choices would your organization make if it were to receive a windfall of $50, $100,000 or $1 million? Does your answer fit into your statement of organizational needs and priorities?

Institutional strategic planning is not easy. Planning efforts absorb time and energy. They often look inward only, are confined by the assumption that the mission is fixed, and produce lengthy reports that gather dust. Nevertheless, for fund-raising purposes (let alone for management and oversight reasons), regular strategic planning should be undertaken. It is up to trustees to see that it is done and done effectively.

4. The Case

Do board members really need to get involved with the case? They do. On the strength of the case will depend fund-raising success; that is reason enough. Moreover, when board members themselves talk about the organization in the community—as well they should, when they recruit fellow board members, when they are asking for support—it is the case they are using.

Yes, trustees should pay attention to the preparation of the case.

Unlike the *mission,* which, as discussed above, is an internal definition of the organization's purposes, programs, and priorities, the *case* has an outward aim toward the public. The case addresses prospective supporters; it sets out in compelling terms the reasons for making a supporting contribution. It interprets and explains the mission for prospective donors, looking at the organization from the supporters' point of view. The case is the "prospectus for investment."

The case need not be a single statement. Rather, it is a concept readily adaptable for use in written proposals, in printed pamphlets, in public meetings, or in any direct, personal solicitation of a gift. The case is couched in the language of persuasion.

But there are wide differences of view about what specifics should go into the case and how it should be formulated. Some insist that it should open with a prestige statement about the organization, giving its age, the respect it enjoys, how many students, patients, beneficiaries, or distinguished admirers it has. But such an initial focus on the organization itself does not address the basic reasons why people make a charitable gift.

It is true that some prominent symphonies, museums, and hospitals have strong bodies of faithful supporters who contribute regularly because of the organization's prestige, but usually giving is not in response to a record of past accomplishment. People give "to make a change for the good." The case for support, therefore, will be stronger if it is based on the focus problem: What is out there in the community that needs doing? Then the case can address what the organization does or will do to meet that focus problem.

A framework, a pattern for articulating the case, is one that addresses the four elements: *Why, What, How,* and *Who.* It goes like this:

1. Begin with the *why.* Why is the organization in business at all? What is the problem, the public's need, that calls for the solutions, the improvements, and the programs the organization provides? What is it that calls for action? Because the case depends so heavily on the *why,* this focus problem needs to be clearly delineated. What are the dimensions of the need, its significance, its ramifications? What happens if the need is not met?

    Response must be more than superficial. Merely to say there is a need for education, entertainment, cultural expression, or health care is insufficient. Get down to cases. What kind of education is not being undertaken or is not achieving a goal, and what results from the shortfall? How bad is the shortage of housing for the poor, and what is its impact on society? If public infant care is sorely deficient, what harms to children and to society result?

2. Only after identifying and explaining the focus problem does the case turn to the *what:* what the organization does to meet the need. What, in simple terms, is the purpose of the program or project, the mission of the organization set up to fill the identified community need? How does the approach differ from what others are doing? (Clearly you frame the *why* to lead up to the *what,* so that the *what* becomes a clear answer to the *why.*)

3. The details of the *what* are left to the *how,* the plan. How will the answer to the focus problem take shape? How will the organization go about its task; how will programs and projects be designed? What are the components, the methodologies? Elaborate on the shape, the impacts, the personnel, the costs, and the plans.

4. Only at its conclusion does the case come to the *who*—who the organization is and how well it has served its constituency and the community. Now, at last, the case may describe briefly the organization's size, history, record, leadership, financing, and support—details that interest the donor but are not the basis for giving.

A summation highlighting the support opportunity, what a contribution will accomplish, can be effective. What specific "change for the good" will a donation make? If "people give to success," here is where the case becomes upbeat and avoids a pleading focus on financial need. Here is where some creative arithmetic can lead to specific examples: X dollars will feed a child one day; Y dollars will place a microscope in the lab or a violin in the studio.

How long should the case statement be? That depends on the uses to which it will be put. The basic concept can usually be covered in two or three pages, single spaced. Once the conceptual base has been articulated (and agreed to by staff and board), it can be adapted to varying uses. As the basic content of a proposal to a foundation or corporation, it will end up in many detailed pages (always with a one-page abstract or executive summary). For a capital campaign, a formal printed and illustrated case statement is customary, probably running to as many as fifteen to twenty pages. But even in these longer formulations, the *why, what, how,* and *who* pattern should be followed.

Building the case for support is too important for the board not to be deeply involved. It is not a job for development staff and executive alone; trustees must themselves come to grips with the formulation of the case, especially if they are to represent the organization in the community and solicit support.

5. The Support Constituency

If the mission is clear and agreed upon and the case for support is persuasive, board members, in putting their attention on fund raising, must turn to the *support constituency;* they must know where the money comes from.

Balancing the budget is a tedium board members sometimes want to leave to management. They shouldn't. Although executive directors must take the initiative and supply the information, trustees must be fully involved; budgets are instruments of planning and of control, both critical to fulfilling board responsibilities. In addition, the *income side* of the budget is where fund raising starts.

The income side of a nonprofit operating financial statement or budget (capital funding is accounted for differently) will show, in basic categories, the following line items:

- *Revenues:* tuitions, admissions, contracts, fees, subscriptions, merchandise sales, and so on
- *Reimbursements:* insurance (such as Medicare/Medicaid) and other reimbursements for services performed
- *Investment income:* income from endowments, bank accounts
- *Unrestricted contributions:* contributions to the institution's operating funds
- *Restricted contributions:* donations and grants to support specific programs and projects

While the proportion of total income to be realized in each category—revenues, reimbursements, investment income, and contributions—is an important part of an organization's overall financial plans, it is the beginning for fund raising. It points up directly the extent of the organization's reliance on contributions to sustain its programs.

The proportional distribution among the categories varies significantly among different types of institutions. Religious organizations, for example, generally receive more than 90 percent of their income from donations, while hospitals take in less than 10 percent from voluntary contributions. Hospital income comes largely from insurance reimbursement revenues (both government and private) and from private payments for services. Among educational institutions, contributions usually constitute about 30 percent of total income, with the other 70 percent coming from tuitions, endowment income, and, for universities, research contracts. To make good fund-raising decisions, a nonprofit organization must carefully study its income proportions by category.

All *contributed* support comes from just five sources:

1. *Individuals:* Perhaps surprisingly, individuals are still the primary source of giving to nonprofit organizations in the United States. Individuals give through membership dues, annual giving, fund-raising benefits, bequests, donated securities and real property, and other means such as family foundations.
2. *Government:* Federal, state, and local agencies make outright grants to nonprofit organizations of all kinds. However, when governments make major contracts or insurance reimbursements for services, the income is considered as revenue earned, not as contributed support.
3. *Business:* Companies give to nonprofit organizations, either directly or through their corporate foundations. (Corporate foundations are simply a conduit for company giving.)
4. *Foundations:* Independent and community (not business or family) foundations of all sizes are a major source of funding for nonprofit institutions.
5. *Nonprofit organizations:* Nonprofit organizations such as churches, professional associations, labor unions, and service

clubs regularly give to other nonprofit institutions, even when such grant making is not their primary mission.

The foregoing are the five sources of contributed income. The ways in which donations are made (the kinds of gifts) can be delineated as follows:

1. *Annual giving:* unrestricted—yearly contributions, memberships, "associates," "friends"
     who gives: individuals, business, other nonprofit organizations
2. *Mass ("direct") mail:* unrestricted
     who gives: individuals
3. *Program/project grants:* restricted—for specific purposes
     who gives: governments, foundations, business, other nonprofit organizations, occasionally individuals
4. *Fund-raising events:* banquets, auctions, sponsored performances, walkathons, and so on
     who gives: individuals, business
5. *Capital funds:* for endowments, buildings
     who gives: individuals, foundations, business
6. *In-kind contributions:* goods or services
     who gives: business, individuals (volunteers)

Putting the sources and the kinds of gifts together, a helpful way of displaying the income pattern for budget and accounting purposes is presented in Exhibit 1. Note that, as capital funds by definition are not part of the operating account, they are not listed. In-kind contributions, while they have monetary value, are generally not shown on the income statement of an operating account; they too must be accounted for separately. Some nonprofit organizations like to record the hours put in by volunteers, including trustees, but as no monetary value can be placed on their work, no figures can be included in accounts or budgets.

Each nonprofit organization will find support from a different array of sources—government, business, foundations, other nonprofit organizations, as well as individuals. An organization may get 80 to 90 percent of its support from a few donors, or it may depend on small gifts from a large number of supporters. The effort

Exhibit 1. Sample Operating Account.

Contributed Income

Source	Unrestricted			Restricted			Totals		
	#	$	%	#	$	%	#	$	%
Individuals		$			$			$	
Government									
Business									
Foundations									
Other nonprofit organizations									
Fund-raising events	___	__		___	__		___	__	
Totals		$	100%		$	100%		$	100%

Revenue Income

Government contracts	(for _____)	$
Government insurance Reimbursements	(for _____)	$
Other insurance Reimbursements	(for _____)	$
Fees	(for _____)	$
Other revenue income	(for _____)	$
Investment income		$ ___
	Total revenue income	$ ___
	Total Income	$

going into the development program, into research, into cultivation and solicitation must reflect these distinctions.

Trustees, if they are to assure that the organization concentrates its fund-raising effort where it will be the most productive, must be clear on the nature and composition of their support constituency.

6. Operating Funds Versus Program Funds

In overseeing the management of institutional finances, trustees need to pay increasing attention to the distinction between *unrestricted* contributions, those that can be used for general operating expenses, and *restricted* donations, those made to fund a specific program or project.

The matter is especially significant because of the current and seemingly growing trend toward giving in support of programs and projects rather than in support of general, unrestricted uses. Government agencies—federal, state, or local—almost without exception restrict their grants and contracts to named programs. Foundations, similarly and increasingly, avoid general institutional support, preferring to direct their grants to those activities that fall within their declared guidelines. Thus nonprofit organizations are forced to look to individuals, businesses, and other nonprofit organizations (religious organizations, service clubs, and labor unions) for unrestricted donations to cover their general operating costs. The trend is such that even businesses are now turning toward restricting their gifts to programs that serve their particular interest.

As a result, both community service organizations and those with a national constituency, while finding it still possible to raise money for a program (restricted funds), are experiencing increased difficulty in raising the unrestricted funds for general operating expenses. Some have fallen dangerously short of funds to cover salaries, rent, and related administrative costs.

Organizations less troubled by this trend toward restricted giving are those that enjoy strong continuing support from a large constituency of individuals and interested corporations. Examples would be advocacy groups, such as those for the environment and wildlife protection; community service organizations such as the Y, the Red Cross, and the American Heart Association; or such established cultural organizations as a symphony or museum—all of which enjoy a long-standing membership roll of loyal givers.

A recent Ford Foundation publication (Seltzer and Cunningham, 1989) highlights the implications for fund-raising programs of this newly emphasized distinction between restricted and unrestricted giving: "Given the fragility of nonprofit funding today, exclusively project-specific support can actually undermine the financial condition of the recipient by contributing to its limbs without attending to its heart." It goes on to say that "the debate is becoming more heated now as nonprofit organizations struggle to pay their bills after government cutbacks and other fiscal threats" [p. 5].

Companies and foundations usually have good reasons for choosing the restricted giving path. Corporate grant makers are under pressure to finance projects with tangible results rather than merely to subsidize organizations. Foundations are often required to follow strict guidelines laid down by a deceased founder.

A further problem arises with foundation grant making. While rightly forcing attention on the end-product service that is going to do the good, foundations have been reluctant to face the fact that overhead costs, organizational infrastructures, are an inextricable and necessarily rising cost of carrying out any project or program. Many foundations even resist paying for overhead costs associated with the programs they are funding. They as much as say, "Do my project, but get someone else to pay the overhead it will need."

Organizations with a zeal for seeking foundation support have thus been known to apply for and accept grants that not only fail to pay for the concomitant administrative costs but even fall short of fully supporting the proposed project. Boards must be alert to the risk that a grant opportunity can bring about a major program disturbance.

Recently a prestigious group of corporate and foundation officials, joined by some representatives of nonprofit receiving organizations, published a report exploring the idea that "corporations and foundations can make grants that will help nonprofits expand their fund-raising capacity—tapping the waiting potential to broaden their bases of support and thus having the means to carry out their missions more effectively." The report states, among other things: "There was general agreement by both grantmakers and providers of technical assistance that any fund-raising grant must be considered in the light of the potential grantee's overall development. Indeed, many felt that once a nonprofit has a sound, well-functioning structure and management, its board and CEO may well be able to learn to raise funds and proceed to do so without any additional outside help. Thus . . . most of the funds for fund raising have gone to smaller (often new) nonprofits in conjunction with grants to develop broad program or management capability" (Baruch College, Department of Public Administration, 1989, p. 6).

Along the same lines, to bridge the restricted-unrestricted chasm, some nonprofit organizations have had success in applying for what they call a Program Development Fund. Enlightened companies, foundations, and philanthropic individuals have come to recognize that fiscally reliable nonprofit organizations, as part of sound management, have a legitimate need for resources to cover constructive expenditures not specially funded. Similar to an institutional reserve, a Program Development Fund is set up to function as quasi-endowment; the yield from investment of the fund is used for project development before funding is at hand. Such a fund may be for innovation and initiatives, or program management, planning, directing, overseeing, accounting, and evaluation. Or it may simply be for legitimate cash flow demands. Frequently it is specified that the principal of the fund can be drawn down only on board authority with a specified replacement plan.

3

Raising Money
from Individuals

The annual report on philanthropy, *Giving USA* (AAFRC Trust for Philanthropy, 1990), estimates total giving from all sources in 1989 to have been $114.7 billion. Of that figure, 84.1 percent, or $96.4 billion, was contributed by individual donors. The figures include gifts to capital campaigns but not bequests, which add another $6.6 billion, to make the total for all individual giving almost 90 percent of all philanthropy. Significantly, but not surprisingly, one half of this high percentage of individual contributions goes to churches, synagogues, and other religious institutions.

Support from individuals comes in various forms: annual giving and memberships; mass direct mail; special events ("fundraisers''); major program and project gifts; and capital gifts, bequests, and planned giving.

The contributions received year in year out from individual supporters in the form of annual giving and memberships, including "associates" and "friends" programs, are a critical source of income for many organizations; for some they are the life's blood. Moreover, campaigns to raise such funds each year serve other important purposes: They bring in the valuable unrestricted funds to pay for operating expenses; they are the best way of identifying the more likely prospects for major project, capital, and planned giving donations; and they are a fine training medium for volunteers, especially trustees.

Mass mailing solicitations are distinguished from annual giving appeals and membership campaigns and are separately discussed.*

Raising money through *special events and benefits,* which also involves individual giving, requires separate organization and procedures.

Major program and project giving by individuals is a different dimension comparable to foundation and corporation giving and is discussed with those subjects. Similarly, individual *capital, bequest,* and *planned giving* are included in the chapters on those subjects.

7. Memberships

Boards of nonprofit institutions spend a lot of time discussing membership matters. Although the question does not arise with all nonprofit organizations, and it is not a subject on which board members need to be expert, trustees should be aware of the different kinds of memberships and the relationship of membership support to annual giving.

---

*The widely used term *direct mail* is misleading in that it confuses two quite different forms of mail solicitation. Here a distinction is made on the one hand between appeals to mailing lists of an institution's own members, supporters, and prospects, as in annual giving, and, on the other hand, mailings to rented, purchased, or exchanged lists of people without prior connection to the organization—that is, "mass mailings."

The concept of membership differs from one type of organization to another. Here, for example, are three types of organizations that use "membership" in quite different ways:*

1. *Professional, trade, and labor associations* exist solely to assist their members to deal jointly with common problems. A bar association, a chamber of commerce, an auto workers union, or a chemists society are examples. Fund raising for them is a straightforward matter of dues collection.
2. *Cultural institutions,* such as theaters, museums, and historical societies, exist to serve the public but have substantial benefits to offer their regular supporters. These cultural organizations have membership programs as cadres of supporters; members give annually, in return for which they receive such benefits as admissions, publications, advance notices, and discounts. Illustrations of this category of membership organization are the National Geographic Society, the Smithsonian Institution, and the Foreign Policy Association—all large national organizations. A local organization such as the Arena Stage in Washington, D.C., with its member associates, is a good illustration of a smaller organization using a membership form of contribution.
3. *Health, welfare, public policy, and other nonprofit organizations,* at both the national and community level, also exist to serve the public but by their nature have no valuable benefits to offer their supporters. They use the device of a "membership" program simply to maintain the loyalty of their annual giving supporters. They can offer few if any benefits beyond newsletters, discounted publications, coffee mugs, or bumper stickers. Environmental organizations, among others, frequently use membership programs, as do local welfare organizations.

Note that it is the benefits that come with membership that distinguish these three categories, which are otherwise not rigor-

---

*The question of "business associates" as a type of membership is discussed separately in Section Thirteen.

ously separated. In the first category, because professional, trade, and labor associations exist only to serve their members, benefits are everything; if members believe they get less than full benefit for their membership dues, they drop out. Although dues tend to be the full extent of the funding of these associations, some create adjunct foundations as an institutional means of raising money to carry out research or other activities beyond what can be expected from dues income. In this way, these associations engage in fund raising apart from their dues collection.

In the second category, while member supporters of cultural and like organizations receive some real benefits—a magazine, lectures, performances—their contributions go well beyond the value of these benefits. The distinction between such membership programs and those of a dues-supported association becomes clear when graduated levels of contributions are invited for virtually the same membership benefits. That doesn't mean the device is deceptive or inappropriate; it simply says that membership is in effect a device to encourage annual giving.

In the third category, where organizations have virtually no significant benefits to offer, the membership device is used to retain the loyalty of the supporters and encourage them to give annually. These organizations might be better advised to invite supporters to become "associates" or "friends" and thus avoid the misleading connotation that special benefits or a vote, customarily associated with membership, are involved.

Some membership programs hardly pay for the token benefits and expense of maintaining the mailing lists and annual solicitation. Still, they may have value simply to supply a prospect list, the collection of names from which later to seek larger contributions. A membership program can thus be useful in attracting future supporters, rather than in drawing immediate support.

Boards of organizations considering membership programs should ask themselves the simple question: members of what? If you cannot visualize participating members deriving rights and special benefits or a vote, normally associated with membership organizations, a membership program may be inappropriate; an "associates" or "friends" program may be more suitable.

Beware, too, of another important possibility. If you set the entrance level for membership at an amount to attract the widest participation, you may invite a minimum contribution from candidates fully capable of giving large annual gifts. People will assume that the minimum amount fulfills their obligation to the cause. An associates or friends program avoids this handicap: Those giving any level of support can legitimately be called "friends" or "associates," where a "membership" should imply benefit for all, without distinction according to size of contribution.

8. Annual Appeals and Phonathons

When annual contributions from regular supporters are the lifeblood of an organization, the appeal deserves the full attention of board members.

Remember that annual giving is not the same as mass mailing to unknown prospects; rather, it is the solicitation each year of a first or repeated donation from preselected individuals who already know, or know about, the organization. But annual giving must be more than mere reminders to members that their dues are due.

Annual giving solicitations are carried out primarily by mail, although churches in their "every member canvas" try to have all parishioners asked in person for donations to match or increase their previous year's contributions. Three cardinal elements count heavily in annual gift solicitations: the *mailing list,* the *appeal letter,* and the *personalized approach.*

Mailing Lists

Although the mailing list is of great importance to other aspects of the organization's communications, it is a central asset to the annual solicitation. Continuous effort must go into broadening the prospective donor base, keeping the list current, and making it useful.

Organization mailing lists are composed of hundreds, even thousands, of names, every one of which, unlike those in mass mailings, is a potential supporter. These are people deliberately selected for the mailing list. They already know the organization, at least by reputation, or know the people associated with it.

Board members can be of great assistance in developing that list. It should hold the names of community leaders and the countless affluent and not-so-affluent people who make up the giving public—people known to the board members. Trustees can make sure their personal address books, business contact lists, club and church rosters, to the extent permitted and appropriate, are all on the organization's mailing list. Names drawn from invitations and annual reports of other organizations and from newspaper articles can all be systematically entered onto an organization's list. But it takes a deliberate, diligent effort to make a strong mailing list.

Keeping the mailing list current is a vital, ongoing, tiresome task. Changes of address or status, spellings, and ZIP Codes all need to be current and correct. People simply do not give to an organization that misspells their name or addresses their late spouse. Returned mail costs time and money. As list maintenance work is routine and generates no deadlines of its own, it can be slighted by a staff caught up in meeting other demands. Ensuring that it is not neglected is a frequent board concern, so board watchfulness, insistence, and provision of labor to do the work are all necessary. Nothing is so useless as a mailing list that is hopelessly out of date.

Exchanging lists with other friendly organizations can be tricky. Once you turn over your list to another institution, you lose control of its use. A good precaution is to offer to send another organization's mailings to your list in return for their doing the same; in that way you keep control. Only responders to such a mailing become legitimately part of your or the other's list.

These days, for all but very small organizations, lists must be on the computer. Even when the computer job is contracted out, the work of updating remains. If you have the hardware, software programs are available to manage the process of entering names, updating data, coding classifications, and giving records. A program will code to distinguish those to whom publications will be sent and those who are to receive any special attentions. Word processors are equipped to print out personally addressed letters. (Computers are discussed further in Section Twenty-Six.)

Trustees need not do all these chores, but it is they who provide the names and the insistence that the tasks get done.

Appeal Letter

You will find strong differences of opinion about appeal letters. One school of thought says that when you reach out to a sophisticated audience your message should be short and to the point: "Nobody reads a lengthy appeal." To another school, experience demonstrates that multipage letters and multiple inserts really work; such mailings bring in a higher percentage of responses. One prominent consultant encourages boards: "Rethink your prejudice against long copy."

Well, the choice is yours. Probably the answer lies in the distinction between the constituency mailings for annual support and the mass, so-called "direct mail" to undiscriminated lists: short, or at least shorter, to the former; long or longer—a more detailed prospectus—to the latter.

In any event, the appeal letter should be a compelling statement making the case for support in language that is warm and personal. If you refer to the earlier discussion of why people give (Section Two), your letter will carry a message of success, not distress, and it will speak of opportunities; your donors will learn about the people you help and those who gain from your service, not about your funding needs. Your letter will point up what change for the good a contribution will make.

Form and layout are important: not a black page of print, short paragraphs, varied margins, underlinings, color (if you have the capacity), but not overly slick. Your letter is competing against many others to get the attention of the reader and to encourage an act of giving. That is a stiff challenge.

Personalized Appeals

Authorities on mail solicitation make two important points about how mailings are seen and responded to. First, they say that people receiving letters of solicitation look first at the salutation (personal or impersonal), next at the signature (Who signs—staff or trustee?

familiar or unfamiliar name?), next at the trustee names on the stationery ("who do we know?"), and next at the P.S. (there is always a P.S.). Only then do they go back to the first sentence and maybe read the letter. Second, experts assert that while you might get a 2 percent response to a "Dear Friend" letter, a "Dear Charlie" letter could bring a 5 to 10 percent reply, and a hand-written note might receive as high as a 20 to 30 percent response.

Those assertions tell you a lot about how you should write your annual appeal for support. They say particularly that you will have far greater success if you can address the letters to the recipient by name, and you can add to that chance if a trustee scribbles a personal note on an otherwise impersonal letter. They show you that the letter should be signed by your board chairman or a well-known friend of your organization. They mandate using stationery with board members' names listed on it. And they encourage you, a trustee, to append a personal, hand-written note, no matter who signs the typewritten letter.

Other Important Matters

Schedules. For annual giving, routines need to be worked out carefully because it takes months to get the tasks in order—mailing lists, the appeal letter, stuffing envelopes, dividing up the writers of personal notes. Organizations differ about optimum times to send letters. Schools and colleges time their appeal to the school year, especially commencement. Other organizations see the late fall as optimum to coincide with popular habits of Christmas and year-end giving. On the other hand, United Way and other metropolitan-coordinated charities may dictate when member agency appeals can go out. Some organizations plan on a follow-up, reminder mailing.

Frequency. How many times during the year can you make an appeal for funds? Again, the answer is different for mass mail solicitations, which seem to be in every mail delivery, and annual giving to a community organization where once, maybe twice a year is probably what the traffic will bear. An appeal made more than once in a year can be identified as the "spring appeal," the "fall appeal," the "Mothers' Day appeal," or, as in some organizations, an appeal related to timely projects.

Giving Levels. It is always desirable to ask someone to consider a higher level of giving, but it is difficult to do so in a general annual appeal. Suggesting alternative levels of a gift—sometimes attaching names to the various levels—is certainly common practice. Here are illustrative arrays of gradations from large to minimal donor:

Benefactor	Senior associate
Patron	Associate
Sponsor	Sponsoring member
Donor	Sustaining member
Contributor	Contributing member
Friend	Member

Larger Gifts. All contributors are important, but those making larger gifts—$500 or more—deserve special attention, as discussed under Cultivation of Prospects (Section Twenty-One), and should be placed in a special category. They should receive more than single, routine acknowledgments; personal reports after a few months showing how their money was spent cannot help but be warmly appreciated. Possibly they should be personally solicited each year. They can belong in a "giving society," if one has been created, and held in readiness for a major program or capital campaign donation.

Giving Societies. A different approach attaches a sense of community to a special group of benefactors. The more generous among regular annual givers can be asked to join an elite group with a contribution of a stated amount: "The President's Club" or another name appropriate to the institution. For some institutions, notably schools and colleges, such giving societies have proven to be a major stimulus for consistent, large gifts by more affluent members of the constituency. Members are always solicited personally and are usually given an appropriate token gift related to the institution.

Acknowledgments. Every donation must be acknowledged, but one must especially not neglect repeat contributors: Loyal annual givers need to receive personal words of appreciation each year. It is difficult to thank someone too often for a gift; those "thank-you's" are the first step in the next solicitation. Givers of large gifts deserve personal letters from a trustee, the chief executive, and the program staff most directly affected. The more prompt and personal the expression of appreciation, the more favorable is the carryover toward further giving.

Phonathons

Although deplored by many in the giving community, phonathons have proven valuable in annual appeals, especially for schools and colleges, but also for community organizations with a loyal following.

Unhappiness with the phonathon device centers on indiscriminate, mass solicitations by unfamiliar organizations that simply follow a telephone book list. People are not inclined to resent a call on behalf of an organization with which they have a connection. Phonathons serve a useful purpose for schools and colleges where the constituency is clear and limited, where "class agents" form a voluntary staff to do the phoning, and where the annual contribution routine is firmly entrenched. Phonathons have proven most effective when they follow directly on a written appeal.

Training, while not difficult, is crucial in mounting a phonathon: The solicitor must follow established routines to avoid putting off the prospect. Unless the phonathon routine is carefully directed, there is danger of doing harm rather than good.

Fair Share Appeals

Occasionally efforts are made to introduce standards or goals to raise the level of individual giving. In some circumstances, notably in church and school appeals, "fair share" tables suggesting the size of gifts have been a useful stimulus. An illustration of a fair share appeal is set out in Exhibit 2.

INDEPENDENT SECTOR, the national association of nonprofit organizations, has its "Fivers" program, summarized by the rubric in IS president Brian O'Connell's New Year's Greeting:

Tithers are the true leaders
of our caring society, but
all of us owe at least five—
five percent of income and
five hours a week—to
the causes of our choice.

Exhibit 2. Sample: Fair Share Giving.

"FAIR SHARE is the annual giving program for . . . parents. Each family is asked to make a voluntary gift to the School—a gift that is fair relative to that family's ability to give.

"Fair Share is the School's priority appeal. Gifts to capital fund drives or to [special events] are sought in addition to, but never in place of, gifts to Fair Share. First and increased gifts to Fair Share will be matched by a [challenge grant].

"Fair Share makes possible for the School to meet important needs without requiring larger increases in tuition. For most parents voluntary contributions are preferable because they are tax deductible and tuition is not."

Gift guidelines for the Fair Share are suggested by the School in the following chart:

Fair Share Guidelines

Income from all sources	Suggested gift to Fair Share
Up to $30,000	$50 to $250
$30,000 to $50,000	$250 to $500
$50,000 to $75,000	$500 to $750
$75,000 to $100,000	$750 to $1,250
$100,000 to $150,000	$1,250 to $2,500
$150,000 to $200,000	$2,500 to $5,000
$200,000 to $300,000	$5,000 to $7,500
Above $300,000	$7,500 to $10,000

A Gift from Every Family.

Source: The Sidwell Friends School, Washington, D.C. Reprinted by permission.

9. Mass Direct Mail

Trustees are susceptible to misleading influences when it comes to mail appeals. They hear of vast sums raised by professionals who successfully mail to thousands of "names." "Why can't we?" they ask. They receive appeals daily themselves—repetitious, insistent, annoying. "There must be money in it," they say. "Otherwise we wouldn't keep getting the stuff."

Some simple truths can help clarify the field of mass direct mail in fund raising.

First, the term *direct mail* is a source of confusion. (Who has heard of indirect mail?) The term applies to mail solicitations sent out to large lists, usually leased from brokers, of names with no known connection with the organization—a deep-sea trawler operation to catch anything it can. What is called direct mail must not be confused with annual appeals and similar mailings, discussed in Section Eight, which go to contributors and known prospects, even though this group may involve a large mailing list.

Almost without exception, successful users of mass mailings are high-profile national organizations, usually with an advocacy mission. Their names and their causes are well known. They have instant recognition of what they are about: National Rifle Association, Gun Control, Planned Parenthood, Right to Life, Common Cause, Save the Children, National Wildlife. Local and regional organizations, even when their mission is readily recognizable, will rarely reach a population sufficiently large to achieve a response worth the expense of a mailing to a mass, undiscriminated list.

The real purpose of mailings to large numbers of unknown names is "list acquisition": You go through the major exercise to get the few responses that then become a part of your constituency, your own list of potential annual givers. In the highly specialized mass mail activity, you are happy with as little as 1 percent positive response to a first mailing. A mass mail program looks two, three, even five years ahead before it reaches a true payoff. You seek to enlarge your donor base because, when people respond, the chances are good that they will continue to give. The payoff comes only after a few years of first-time responders giving repeatedly.

Although with favorable conditions mass mail programs can

be highly successful, especially for large national organizations, a poorly prepared program is doomed. Retaining specialists and responding to careful cost-benefit experience are requisites. Success depends on acquiring good lists from list brokers who rent for one-time use. (Lists are usually rented, not purchased; you pay again for a second mailing from a rented list. Names become yours only when they respond with a contribution.)

The lists, available at minimums of 5,000 or 10,000 names, are highly categorized for specialized uses: by ZIP Code (discriminating between affluent and nonaffluent zips), by income level, by age, by known or suspected interests such as the environment or refugees, by political or religious leaning—even by attitudes on quite specific issues such as abortion or gun control.

Is your organization able to make good use of such sophisticated techniques? If not, the cost is prohibitive.

If the foregoing presents a discouraging picture for the typical local, educational, welfare, community service organization, it is meant to. If it points back to the need to put strong emphasis on developing the organization's own mailing list, that too is intended. Mass mail fund raising has high risks and no shortcuts. Programs call for money to be invested when the chances of appreciable return are hard to evaluate. That is reason enough for boards to get involved in mass mail decisions.

10. "Benefits" and Other Fund-Raising Events

Some people associated with nonprofit organizations think of fund raising solely in terms of "benefits"—special events put on to raise money. They have seen in the newspapers how banquets, balls, auctions, sporting events, and theater performances—usually with prominent names involved—bring in major financial support. Perhaps they have participated in such a gala for a favorite charity. To them, that is what fund raising is all about. Trustees need to be realistic and deliberate, however, about this aspect of fund raising.

It is true, some institutions mounting major fund-raising events enjoy great success, year after year. Certainly the number of such "fundraisers" in every city attests to their popularity. In addition to their financial gain, benefits can have important public relations value, raising the profile of the organization, involving more people, and, as is often heard, "having fun, too." Nevertheless, a prudent board will weigh carefully all financial and other costs and gains before deciding to undertake such an event.

Don't confuse fundraisers with special events put on for cultivation of prospective major donors or to celebrate success. With them direct fund raising is not involved. Money is not asked for; the organization pays the way. Such events are used for the "kick off" of capital campaigns or for annual dinners honoring special "patron clubs." They perform functions important to fund raising but are quite distinct from fund-raising benefits.

Here are some of the principal cautions, aspects of this kind of fund raising that call for special attention.

Benefits are labor intensive, usually eating up huge amounts of board, staff, and volunteer time. That is the principal reason why *leadership* should be at the top of the list of considerations. You need to be assured, before you commit, that you have a person or a group to take hold and run the project. Good ideas will abound, but failing the leadership, you tie up both board and staff in discussions, frustrations, and the detailed work it takes to pull off the event. Event leaders can come from the board, or, better yet, from strong volunteers, but leaders there must be.

Closely following leadership, *volunteers* must be recruited. The time and effort fundraisers demand must not fall on the staff, who are busy enough with programs and administrative duties. Professional managers, "arrangers" of such benefits and occasions, can be found who, for a fee, will take over much of the detailed workload, but they do not replace the need for strong leadership and volunteer support. Too often community organizations embark on fund-raising events assuming that staff or board members will carry the load, only later to find the burden to be far more than was anticipated. Line up the committee first—the chiefs and the Indians.

The *budget* for an event is frequently difficult to formulate. Income, of course, will depend on the price set and the highly speculative estimate of expected attendance. The costs can be manifold and slippery—programs, promotions, invitations, food, service, and so on—much of it determined by the unclear numbers expected and the supplies and services that will be donated by friendly vendors. The break-even point will depend on the difficult calculation of expected participants at the price you set. If, as often happens, the actual results do not show a gain, the effort was not worthwhile. You will benefit in fellowship and public relations, but that's no fundraiser.

Beware of *constituency conflict:* You may be asking for a contribution, sponsorship, or attendance of the same individuals and corporations who make up your strongest annual giving support. They may be reluctant to do both, and it's dangerous to expect board members to be taxed to support every benefit an organization mounts.

Look out for the *competition.* Other nonprofit organizations in your community are walking the same path, designing similar events at similar times, appealing to the same people. It may be possible to find out what others are planning, but unexpected conflict can be ruinous.

Then there is the matter of *repetition.* Events do need years to grow, to become established. If yours earns a substantial sum for your operating budget, will you be willing to repeat the effort each year? If not, how will you fill the income gap its absence leaves?

Finally, the *tax-deduction* question is tricky. Although federal and local authorities make available information on rules for deductions, it is not always clear how specific an organization must be in declaring what part of the subscription to an event is tax deductible. The responsibility for claiming tax deduction apparently lies with the donor, but event sponsors have to be cautious not to declare subscription to an event as tax deductible without subtracting the fair market value of anything received—the meal or any items bought at auction. Even raffle tickets, where they are legal, appear not to be tax deductible.

Although boards should be cautious about fund-raising events, they should by no means avoid them entirely. Small and large organizations have been able to build up traditional or novel events that become important income sources and have significant public relations advantages. Banquets, dances, cruises, auctions, rummage sales, walkathons, and theater and movie first nights have raised major support for nonprofit organizations of every kind. Volunteer leaders are out in the community willing and able to bring off such successful fundraisers. Through volunteer enthusiasm, wide interest leading to support can be generated.

As a trustee, when the subject of fund-raising events comes up, just be careful and have your eyes open.

4

Raising Money
from Other Sources

11. Government Grants

Federal, state, county, and municipal agencies make grants to non-profit organizations quite apart from their contracts for services. Boards must be aware of such government assistance because to some institutions it can be a major segment of a budget and because of the troubles and risks that attend receiving such grants.

Staff members carrying out substantive programs are generally knowledgeable about the availability of government grants. Through their professional associations, museum directors are aware of the Institute of Museum Sciences, and visual and performing artists know the National Endowment for the Arts, even as physical and social scientists, researchers, and educators are familiar with the National Endowment for the Humanities and the National Science Foundation. Agricultural economists know the Department of Agriculture and foresters the Bureau of Land Management. Those who don't know of these potential sources of government support have only to turn to the *Government Assistance Almanac,* the comprehensive annual "Guide to All Federal Financial and Other Domestic Programs" (Washington, D.C.: Foggy Bottom Press).

At the state and local level, government grants are found in all community service fields—health, welfare, housing, culture, and recreation.

The troubles attending government assistance are essentially bureaucratic—interminable delays and endlessly complex paperwork—but they can raise doubt that the grant is worth the effort. Nor is there any single system, right path, or short route through the troubles; each agency is one of a kind with its own forms, rules, and personalities. But these troubles are the concern of staffs, not of boards.

The risks are of a particular kind. A nonprofit organization can become overdependent on government grants and contracts. Governments are fickle and politics are volatile. And to governments, contracts are not sacred: They may be binding on the nonprofit signer, but they can be cut off without recourse or prior notice by a government agency. An organization with commitments made on the basis of a revocable grant can find itself suddenly in deep financial difficulty.

In seeking government support, the trustee's role is generally limited. Occasionally a board member, through personal contacts, can ease the way to a grant-making official and assure a full hearing on a proposal. But in the main, the board can confine its work to overseeing the government assistance aspect of the organization's finances.

12. Foundation Grants

According to the 1990 edition of *Giving USA* (AAFRC Trust for Philanthropy, 1990), America's independent and community foundations, excluding those serving as adjuncts to corporations, granted an estimated $6.7 billion in 1989 to charitable and other nonprofit organizations, representing 5.8 percent of total giving for the year.

The distribution pattern of foundation grants is of interest to boards. According to the *Foundation Grants Index* of the Foundation Center (1989), grants were distributed in roughly the following division:

Welfare*	27%
Health	20.2%
Education	17.1%
Cultural activities	14.5%
Social science	9.8%
Science	9.3%
Religion	2%

As with other fund raising, securing foundation support involves careful preparation and deliberate asking, in both of which trustees can be helpful. Because grants from foundations may be an important part of the institution's contributed income, trustees should be fully aware of the techniques and should from time to time participate in the process, especially when they know the foundation officials.

It is important to be clear on just what is covered in this discussion on foundation support and what is not. Not included are the following:

- *Government foundations*, such as the National Science Foundation and the National Endowments for the Humanities and the Arts, which clearly belong in the category of Government Grants (Section Eleven)
- *Company-sponsored foundations*, such as Exxon Foundation and General Electric Foundation, which, as they are simply

*Includes, among other areas, community affairs, crime and law enforcement, environment and energy, and rural and urban development.

conduits for company philanthropy, follow the pattern of Business Donations (Section Thirteen) rather than that of independent foundations (a distinction on which nonprofit organizations frequently are confused)

- *Operating foundations,* such as the Kettering Foundation and the J. Paul Getty Trust, which use their resources mainly to conduct research, maintain facilities, or provide direct service with their grants related directly to their own operating program

- *Adjunct foundations,* such as the University of Maryland Foundation and the Children's Hospital of San Francisco Foundation, which are nonoperating, non-grant-making entities created by such institutions as state universities, hospitals, or professional and trade associations as facilities to raise and manage money in support of the parent organization

- *Family foundations,* technically classified as "independent foundations," whose decisions are made by the donor, the donor's family, or a trust officer acting on the donor's behalf, with grants more logically considered as individual giving.

Foundation support does consist of grants from *independent foundations,* organizations established to aid social, educational, religious, or other charitable activities as determined by an independent board of governors or trustees, and *community foundations,* publicly sponsored organizations deriving funds from various donors and making grants in a specific community or region as determined by a board representing the diversity of the community.

The seemingly small share—less than 7 percent—of all philanthropy coming from this strictly defined foundation segment can be deceptive. In fact, these grants can be sizable, into the many thousands of dollars. Not only can independent and community foundation grants represent a major supporting element in a nonprofit's financial picture but a single foundation grant can equal hundreds of individual contributions, the raising of which would absorb great organizational effort.

Asking for support from a foundation differs from other types of fund-raising appeals in the following ways:

- With foundations, more than with corporations and government agencies, long-term relationships are at once possible and desirable; an accepted proposal is likely to be a beginning, not an end.
- Personal communications with staff or board members can often be made before a proposal is submitted; in some circumstances, foundation collaboration on the preparation of the proposal is even possible. After the proposal is submitted, personal support directed to a foundation official by an influential volunteer, especially a board member, is useful, if handled tactfully.
- Although many foundations like to share support of a program or project with other foundations, they want to know about it and make deliberate decisions. Submission of the same proposal, simultaneously and without acknowledgment, to more than one foundation is not recommended.
- You can usually determine why a proposal was turned down and plan to submit a revised version. When your proposal is turned down, you do yourself no harm in thanking the foundation for sympathetic consideration of your proposal.

Preparation

Preparation is a matter of research and selection. Happily, extensive facilities, notably the Foundation Center, are available with the needed information, though time and effort must be put into the task. The center publishes the *Foundation Directory,* comprehensively and systematically listing foundations, their interests and guidelines, their giving patterns, and the names of their officials. In addition, the directory classifies foundations by declared interest in each of the important fields of philanthropic endeavor. The center's libraries contain the income tax returns (IRS Form 990) on each foundation, showing the actual grants made. The center also makes available services for searching out grant-making information in the foundation field and copious reference books, periodicals, and other materials.

The selection part of the preparation involves matching your organization's funding needs with the declared interests and guidelines of the various foundations. This is where the work is. Of the more than 6,000 foundations with assets of $1 million or more (which account for 87 percent of all foundation grant making), many are regional, in that their giving is restricted to a specific area, or specialized, in that their grants are confined to certain fields of interest—educational, religious, cultural. Some have policies forbidding grants to endowments or to buildings. The asker must know the facts.

Although in the main it is a staff's function to do the preparatory research, board members can be helpful. A personal contact with a foundation board or senior staff member will at a minimum assure a sympathetic hearing. When a foundation calls for an interview, again a board member's presence will be valuable, if for no other reason than to demonstrate the board's involvement.

Asking

If research has been done and a personal contact has not been found, how do you get the foundation's attention? Sending in a full proposal unannounced rarely gets a positive response; somehow you have to attract interest.

In recent years a sensible procedure has been developed, initiated by the John D. and Catherine T. MacArthur Foundation of Chicago and now followed by others. A nonprofit organization is invited to submit a *memorandum* of not more than two pages describing the program for which funding is sought. The foundation can then, if it is interested, ask for a full proposal. Nonprofit organizations can use this helpful procedure when taking initiative toward a foundation new to it. But, as John E. Corbally, former president of the MacArthur Foundation, said, "Look for a fit. Don't try to create one where it doesn't exist."

Care must go into the preparation of the memorandum itself. It will have a short covering letter inviting the foundation's attention, pointing out the coincidence of interest with the foundation's guidelines. It should ask to be considered for a grant of a stated amount. The memorandum will be a succinct statement of the case to be made for a program, following the prescription (Section Four) for preparing the case. It will articulate the focus problem, the missing element in the community, or the nation, or the world—the *why* of the program—before it speaks to *what* the program is or does and *how* it does it. Only in the end will it briefly describe the organization itself and its record, or, better yet, enclose an annual report.

The foundation is going to make the grant, if it does, not because the organization is outstanding but because the program for which a supporting grant is sought will "make a change for the good." The case statement memorandum should therefore make clear at the outset what it is that needs doing, what change for the good is called for, even before it talks about the proposed program and the organization. And it should do this *all in two pages.*

The culmination of the process of solicitation, unless the foundation chooses to make a site visit, is the preparation and submission of a proposal, a topic to be developed in Section Fifteen, Proposal Writing.

Again, although staff will be responsible for preparing a proposal, board members should oversee and support it, ensuring that presentations are as compelling as possible. It may well be a board function to present the cover letter inviting the foundation's attention and pointing out the shared interest with the foundation's guidelines.

13. Business Donations

Giving USA, 1990 (AAFRC Trust for Philanthropy, 1990), reports that corporations and corporate foundations donated an estimated $5 billion to charitable and other nonprofit causes in 1989, representing 4.4 percent of total giving for the year.

The distribution of corporate donations (*Giving USA, 1989,* using a Conference Board Survey of 356 companies, reporting 1988 rounded figures) was as follows:

Health and Human Services	29.2%
Education	37.3%
Culture and Art	11.1%
Civic and Community	12.9%
Other	11.1%

While this corporate share of total philanthropy seems small in comparison with individual giving (90 percent), it does compare well with foundation grants (5.8 percent). For many organizations, corporate donations can be a significant part of their income picture; boards must ensure that the corporate solicitation program is in good order. On the other hand, it is not uncommon for trustees to exaggerate the potential; they too hastily assume that companies have limitless public relations coffers.

Make no mistake, however: Board members are the key element in most successful solicitation of business support.

But first a negative note. Frequently a board member will undertake to solicit corporate donations simply by writing personal letters to senior executives. You can hear the member say, "I know these fellows. They should give to us. A few of them owe me one. I'll sign some letters." It doesn't work. Companies are sophisticated in their philanthropy; solicited by hundreds of institutions, all worthy, they do not react favorably to letters, even from personal friends. It is too easy for them to ask their contributions officer to draft a response, and too easy to find reasons for saying no gracefully, even to friends.

Mail solicitations are appropriate for renewals, asking a company to contribute its annual support, thanking them for past support, and reporting on activities. Otherwise, letter solicitations to companies are right *only* when other strategies are not available. When corporate leaders have successfully raised large sums for nonprofit organizations, they have done so by diligent personal contact, perhaps "picking up some IOU chips" from their own past contributions; they have not done it by simply writing letters.

What, then, is the best way to solicit contributions from the business community? As with appeals for individual gifts, successful strategies for corporate fund raising call for much effort in *research and selection, preparation,* and establishing orderly, reliable *procedures.*

Research and Selection

Hundreds and hundreds of companies—industries, banks, service and professional firms, developers and builders, media, and others—are prospects for support of any nonprofit organization. A fund-raising strategy, therefore, must start with extensive and thorough research to glean all possible information on the likely companies, their products and services, their location, their giving habits, and, most important, the identity of their decision-making officials.

Such information comes from directories (including *Standard and Poor's, Dun and Bradstreet,* and others) and local board of trade listings, available by subscription or in libraries; from company annual reports; from asking others; and even from calling the company and asking key questions. Be sure to tap your own board members from the business community.

Selecting the companies to approach and setting priorities among them is important because it leads to putting time and effort where the prospects are best, where the money is. In making this selection, it pays to apply the following criteria:

1. Has the company *contributed before?* The best prospect is one that has given before.
2. Is the company known otherwise to be a *generous giver?* It can be a waste to spend time on those known to be limited in their philanthropy. Some companies do not have organized giving programs; they may even have a policy precluding corporate giving. Research can tell you.
3. Can you identify a *personal contact?* Since "people give money to people," finding a personal contact with an official of a company will often make the difference in getting a donation; it is absolutely necessary for a major contribution.
4. Is there a *mutual interest* served by what the organization does? Companies give money out of good corporate citizenship, but they also give where they see direct or indirect company interest. It is important to identify this interest as part of the selection process and to guide the ultimate solicitation.

Although company gifts are usually cleared through a contributions committee or officer, or through a corporate foundation, solicitations can be initiated through an operating, marketing, or

public relations division when a company has a direct interest in
the activities of the nonprofit organization.

Preparation

Careful preparation for each solicitation involves the determination
of the following:

1. *Who is the person to see* in the prospective company? Although
    it is assumed you will seek out the highest official with whom
    a contact can be made, it pays to keep other company officials
    informed. You may not get in to see the senior company offi-
    cial, even with a friendly introduction, but the top officer may
    pass you along to the contributions officer, who will take more
    notice of you because the boss said so.
2. *Who is the best person to make the solicitation?* Select the
    person who will command the greatest respect in the eyes of the
    official to be visited. The first person to volunteer may not be
    the best one to solicit the gift. Find the best, because success will
    hang on that selection. Two people may be better than one, but
    not more unless you are meeting with a group.
3. *How much do you ask for?* Always request a stated amount.
    You may not get what you ask for but you won't get turned
    down for naming an amount you want the company to con-
    sider, and you will set the sights.
4. *What case do you make?* Corporations are obliged to justify
    charitable giving to their stockholders. Clearly you want to
    cater to the interests of the company. Your preference will be
    for an unrestricted, institutional grant: "If you like what we are
    doing, give us operating money." But the company's interest
    may be in a particular program or project.

Although these guidelines for preparation may sound like
commonplace, textbook fund raising, they are what count in seeking the corporate dollar. And again, it is trustees who are invaluable
in the process: they are the ones who have the knowledge of the
business world and the acquaintances who are the entrées.

In making the key decision about who should do the asking,

the preferred choices are these. The first choice clearly is to have a member of the board make the solicitation, in person, with or without accompanying staff or other board member. The second choice is to have a board member make the introduction for the chief executive or staff member who will call on the company. The third choice is for the chief executive or a staff member to seek an appointment to see the contributions officer. The fourth choice is for a board member to make a telephone call to be followed by a proposal letter. A fifth choice is to send a letter of solicitation, a poor choice even when it is addressed to the company CEO and personally signed by the chairman of the board.

What if you can't find any contact with a company official? Is everything lost? By no means. You will have to resort to a letter, but it will be a different kind of appeal than having the chairman write a "Dear Bill" letter to the company CEO. You will follow the same course as with the approach to a foundation (Section Twelve). Prepare a short, compelling case statement memorandum (not a full proposal) on your organization or the project for which you are seeking support. Send it with an even shorter covering letter, probably to the company contributions officer, pointing out the common interest you share and what kind of support you are seeking and offering to visit or send in a full proposal. It may not work, but you are making the best stab at it.

Look at it this way: If you were the company official, what kind of approach would you find interesting? Follow your answer as a guide.

Procedures

To carry out adequate research for the selection and preparation process, you will do well to have a file for each prospective company, into which every scrap of possibly relevant information is put. The file should be built upon a study of directory information and interviews with others, including especially knowledgeable board members. The key is that *all* information, including the seemingly trivial, goes into the file. A computerized filing system may be helpful for basic information and gift records, but an old-fashioned file folder for each prospect is still necessary.

In addition, each corporate prospect should have a *profile sheet,* a single page capable of ready reproduction for review in the selection and preparation processes. On it systematically show the names of key officials (probably copied from a directory); the names of all potential contacts; and a simple chronology of correspondence, visits, and giving record. Profile sheets can be assembled in notebooks organized by geographic location, by type of business, alphabetically, or by priority.

Systems should be established to ensure

- A follow-up of every asking; a thank-you for the visit; a confirmation of any action or proposal (in addition, personal supporting letters that can be sent by board members)
- Prompt acknowledgments and letters of appreciation for contributions (people can't be thanked too often)
- Timely renewal requests
- Reporting regularly to contributors by newsletter or annual report to keep them interested

Over time, comprehensive, orderly, reliable procedures will make for successful fund raising; conversely, either inept procedures or careless application of sound procedures can hurt the best of research, preparation, and asking.

To enlist the support of business, some organizations create a "business advisory council" or "corporate circle" with members drawn from several sectors of the business and professional community. Members of such a council are asked to advise on approaches to business for contributions, to make introductions, and to assist in solicitations. Contributions from council members' companies are of course expected. Although it is not easy to establish such councils and to recruit members, they can be helpful. The nonprofit board, however, must be clear in its own mind that it is not passing responsibility for fund raising to an outsider group; it is enlisting help.

The involvement of individual board members, especially those on a board development committee, is the crux of a successful corporate fund-raising program. Board members play a key role in

each of the foregoing elements of the corporate fund-raising strategy. They have the information with which to make intelligent
selection of prospects. They are in the best position to guide in the
preparation. And, as the peers of the company officials to be solicited, they can be invaluable in making personal solicitations or
accompanying staff visits.

14. Support from Other Nonprofit Organizations

Certain nonprofit organizations other than foundations are char-
tered under tax laws to give to charity. The United Way and the
Combined Federal Campaign fall into this category; so also do synagogues and churches of all denominations, labor unions, professional associations, and service clubs and associations such as
Rotary and Kiwanis. The Junior League not only makes institutional grants to deserving organizations but contributes volunteer
workers.

The giving potential of this sector of the philanthropic
world is frequently overlooked. This is unfortunate because its potential has three dimensions: An appeal to a religious organization,
service club, or professional association may elicit a donation from
the organization itself; it may offer an attractive opportunity for
individual contributions from its members; and it may produce
volunteers.

The United Way and other combined campaigns have special rules. Member organizations that receive funding support from
them must limit their fund-raising activities to certain times of the
year and to certain categories of grant support.

An effective means of reaching out to these nonprofit grant-
making groups, including churches and synagogues, is through a
speakers' bureau to supply informed, entertaining speakers to fo-
rums and luncheon or dinner meetings. Not only may the organization make a grant but, again, the interest of individual members
may be stimulated, and new prospects may be identified.

Trustees can assist materially in this sector by both making
contacts and giving speeches. The board should assure that a constructive approach is made to invite support from other nonprofit
organizations.

15. Proposal Writing

Although proposal writing is a staff activity, board members should know the difference between a good and a poor proposal. They can help make a good one.

Experts in proposal writing are a dime a dozen: It is one of those skills in which everyone believes no one else can be more proficient. Nevertheless, here are a few suggestions to help board members evaluate a proposal:

1. A proposal is no more nor less than the case tailored to a particular donor. Look at the case through the eyes of that donor; then write a prospectus of that donor's investment. Avoid the temptation to write about your organization's need.

2. Whether long or short, detailed or summary, whether asking for support of an institution, a program, or a project, the proposal should follow the lines of the case statement as earlier (Section Four) described in detail:

- Start with the focus problem. *Why* is there need for what the organization or program does? What is missing that needs to be addressed? "People give money to make a change for the good"; what is that needed change?
- Explain *what* the organization or program does to meet that societal need.
- Say something about *how* the program is structured—perhaps some overall cost, personnel, and timing information, though details can go into appendixes.
- End with *who* the organization is, telling just enough to be convincing on the score of competence. Again, grants are not made because the institution is worthy but because something needs doing and your organization is going to do it.

3. Avoid padding. Government, corporate, and foundation officials are professional; they can distinguish substance from rhetoric. Especially avoid currently overused words, today's clichés, and what has come to be known as "the baffle-gab thesaurus," such as:

unique	catalyst
most unique (!)	bottom line
outreach	critical mass
facilitate	meaningful
in-depth	prioritize
maximize	networking
dialogue	conceptualize

4. If the proposal is more than four or five pages, include an abstract, an executive summary of the *why, what, how,* and *who,* on no more than one page. Staffs of the donor organizations will summarize proposals for their chiefs; better it be your summary than theirs.

5. Make good use of appendixes; they reduce the bulk of the proposal and make it more readable. Budgets can be in an appendix.

6. Form is as important as content. A proposal that stands by itself with a short covering letter is better than a long letter-proposal. It can be more comfortable to put the money request in the covering letter rather than in the proposal. The proposal can make clear an overall budget, of which only a part may be requested. Don't "blacken" the page. Margins, spacing, paragraphing can make an attractive presentation.

5

Raising Capital Funds: The Board's Special Responsibility

Trustees, like all who are concerned with fund raising, need to keep in mind the fundamental distinction between asking for contributions to support the program and ongoing operations, on the one hand, and asking for capital contributions for building or endowment, on the other. The two are quite different.

Capital giving for endowments and buildings includes three types of gifts, each of which is discussed separately: outright donations and pledges, usually in *capital campaigns; planned giving and bequests;* and *life insurance contributions.* But first some general observations on capital giving.

Government agencies and nonprofit grant-making organizations are not usually interested in capital giving. Corporations and foundations infrequently give to capital campaigns for endowments, although some do give to buildings. Although there are important exceptions, capital giving, for the most part, focuses on individuals.

Capital gifts can be thought of as at least ten times the size of annual gifts. People give in annual contributions and memberships from their *current income*. They give to capital funds from their *personal capital*. That personal capital will have come from inherited money, accumulated wealth from successful business ventures, or from disposable income arising from the sale of personal property marked by unusual capital gains. The source of capital holdings, together with the sense of obligation to heirs, will influence the manner in which donors make their gifts: *outright donation* or pledge, *planned giving* or bequest, or *life insurance contribution*.

Raising capital funds to meet building or endowment needs is best accomplished by setting up a structure with a goal, a timeline, and a volunteer organization. But even when you are not embarked on such a capital campaign, it is well not to overlook opportunities to cultivate and solicit major donations, be they special one-time program gifts or capital grants. Opportunities do arise quite apart from any formal campaign, and board members are the ones to spot them. Trustees and development staffs need to be alert to identify loyal, enthusiastic, and affluent supporters who, when the time is right and an attractive project is put before them, will take pleasure in making a substantial gift. An ongoing, low-key capital fund program always takes advantage of opportunities for capital giving even when no expensive and complex campaign is under way.

Trustees need to be cautious about four aspects of capital gift solicitation:

1. *Comparisons are dangerous.* Your organization, capability, and potential are not like any other. You cannot look at what another, seemingly similar institution has done and expect it to be the same for you with your own strengths, constituency, case, and leadership. Nor can you base estimates on your previous record; organizations and circumstances change. Be as objective as you

can in making all the difficult decisions leading to major gift solicitations.

2. *"Averaging" is deceptively simple.* "If we are to reach a goal of $1 million, why not find one hundred prospects to give $10,000 each and avoid the burden of mounting a full-fledged campaign?" It doesn't work that way. Experience clearly demonstrates that you need to approach at least three or four prospects for each gift received; that means finding three or four hundred prospects, not just one hundred, for the $10,000 donations. That's a different proposition. Moreover, limiting the amount you ask for to any figure sets a ceiling that cuts off a chance for the larger gift; people rarely give more than they are asked for. To achieve an *average* of $10,000, therefore, you need to ask for many gifts at a higher level. In major campaigns it is the leadership gifts, not the average ones, that take you to your goal.

3. *Does raising capital funds interfere with annual giving?* Development officers can be reluctant to seek capital funding lest it threaten the regular solicitation of annual contributions. Although they are right in the short run—a capital campaign can divert annual giving while it is in progress—experience shows that capital campaigns reinforce annual giving by broadening the appeal, infusing enthusiasm, and generally raising the attention given the organization. There is never a "right time" to mount a capital campaign, but when capital funds are needed, a campaign interference with annual giving will have to be lived with and overcome in the long run.

A related dilemma always emerges: whether to wrap the annual giving into the capital campaign goal or have annual giving appeals proceed separately while the campaign is under way. You can argue either way, but most professionals, in the absence of special circumstances, come down on the side of including the annual giving in the campaign goal.

4. *Anniversaries do little for capital fund raising.* "For our upcoming twentieth anniversary, why don't we mount a major capital campaign?" Although anniversaries make for good promotion, they are *not* an incentive for giving. Make as much fuss as you can about the anniversary, attract as much favorable attention as you can, but do not expect that donors are going to be moved to give

your organization a capital-size gift as a tenth, or even fiftieth, birthday present. If they give, if will be for the charitable reasons earlier discussed. Even when successful campaigns are tied to an anniversary, their success is not to be attributed to it. So, exploit anniversaries as a cultivation device, but don't count on them to attract money.

16. Capital Campaigns: Endowments and Buildings

Every nonprofit organization will, at one time or another, have need for capital funds for endowment or for building. It's inevitable. Boards will always wish they could once and for all raise an income-earning fund that would produce enough to cover basic operating expenses and remove that constant cash flow pressure. But neither normal revenues nor contributions can be expected to cover such major capital needs. For endowments and for buildings, even for extensive renovation, special capital fund-raising efforts must be undertaken.

Because people being asked to make capital-sized gifts will be drawing on *their* capital—their savings, securities, or real property—special plans are required. You need a separate case statement, research, goal, timeline, and volunteer organization. You need a capital campaign with its own structure and an exceptional commitment and effort by board, chief executive, and staff.

How can you tell whether or not your organization is ready for such an effort? How can you be realistic about a formidable goal involving far more money than you have ever asked for before?

You can't get a clear-cut answer. You always fall back on a balanced judgment resulting from deliberate, risk-taking decisions of the board. The determination usually calls for the help of outside professional assistance.

You need to consider

- A clear analysis of the *funding needs*
- A compelling *case*
- A realistic judgment of the *potential* to raise such capital funds
- An objective evaluation of the *readiness* of the organization to mount such a large undertaking
- A comprehensive *plan* for proceeding

Funding Needs

Organizations go astray by confusing *funding needs* with *fund-raising potential*. Each is crucial to a capital campaign but the two are not the same.

When an organization is thinking about a capital campaign, its first step is to establish what it needs money for and how much has to be raised. This must not be guesswork or simply a "wish list." To be soundly based, funding needs should emerge from thorough, exacting, long-term, or strategic planning, which often requires several months of intensive effort by board and staff working together. Both must explore, with as much objectivity as they can marshal, where they want their organization to go and why.

The best planning usually starts by speculating on the probable future conditions, the environment in which the organization will need to operate in the next ten to twenty years. Then follows a determination of the purposes, programs, and priorities the organization will want to pursue to live most effectively in that projected environment. Estimates of facilities and personnel needed to fulfill the future desired status will be dependable; the dollar figures emerging from the analysis will be the funding needs.

Case

To raise capital funds, a case statement must be prepared setting out why people should make a major donation, what opportunity is presented by the proposed building or endowment for which the money is being sought. Here, even as with the case for operating and program funds, the case must point to the opportunities presented, what needs for change exist in the community, and what will be the result upon completion of the program. A general appeal "to help out the financial needs" of the organization is insufficient. The pattern of *why, what, how,* and *who,* outlined in Section Four, should be followed just as rigorously for a capital campaign.

Capital campaign case statements will contain the following information:

- A summary
- A brief statement of the organization's mission
- A convincing description of the purposes to which the capital funds will be put, together with the funding needs associated with each purpose
- Something about ways one can give—pledges, gifts of securities, or gifts of real property
- Recognition opportunities—buildings, rooms, or scholarships to be named for donors
- Lists of names: the board and campaign leadership

The presentation as a whole should be attractive. Pictures help. Your case statement is your vehicle to convince people that their support is worthwhile.

Potential

Here is the difficult part. Although with deliberate effort you can become reasonably sure about your funding needs, evaluating the potential of successfully raising funds for such a different order of magnitude than you are used to is extremely difficult. It is highly judgmental when you go to estimating the strength of your support constituency for giving capital donations. From whom will the money come? What size will contributions be? To be realistic, capability, not need, must determine your goal.

That this evaluation of potential is critical becomes clear when you consider some well-tested maxims of capital fund drives: 90 percent of your goal will come from 10 percent of your contributors; one lead gift will cover between 10 and 20 percent of your goal; 40 to 50 percent of your total will come from the ten highest givers.

These figures from experience have led to the formation of standard "Tables of Needed Gifts," also known as "Contributions Pyramids." Examples of these pyramids are seen in Exhibit 3.

How then do you adequately evaluate the strength of your support constituency, your potential? Insider board and staff guesses as to donor potential are merely that—guesses, sheer speculation without objective base or reliability.

Exhibit 3. Capital Campaigns: Sample Contributions Pyramids.

For a $2 Million Campaign

1 gift	$ 500,000	=	$	500,000
1 gift	250,000	=		250,000
3 gifts	100,000	=		300,000
5 gifts	50,000	=		250,000
10 gifts	25,000	=		250,000
20 gifts	10,000	=		200,000
40 gifts	5,000	=		200,000
Other gifts				50,000
			$	2,000,000

For an $8 Million Campaign

1 gift	$ 1,000,000	=	$	1,000,000
1 gift	750,000	=		750,000
3 gifts	500,000	=		1,500,000
5 gifts	250,000	=		1,250,000
6 gifts	100,000	=		600,000
10 gifts	50,000	=		500,000
30 gifts	25,000	=		750,000
75 gifts	10,000	=		750,000
100 gifts	5,000	=		500,000
200 gifts	1,000	=		200,000
Other gifts				200,000
			$	8,000,000

For a $25 Million Campaign

1 gift	3,000,000	=	3,000,000
4 gifts	1,000,000	=	4,000,000
8 gifts	500,000	=	4,000,000
15 gifts	250,000	=	3,750,000
30 gifts	100,000	=	3,000,000
60 gifts	50,000	=	3,000,000
100 gifts	10,000	=	1,000,000
300 gifts	5,000	=	1,500,000
Other gifts			1,750,000
		$	25,000,000

The alternative is to perform what is known as a *feasibility study*. A carefully structured survey is undertaken with confidential and noncommitting interviews—perhaps as few as thirty or as many as seventy—with friends and supporters of the organization. By such "testing of the waters," objective data reveals, although not definitively, the degree of community and constituency respect for and commitment to the organization. Such surveys give a reasonably reliable evaluation of the base upon which such a capital campaign will lie and present a rationale for a goal determination, which can then be compared with the need determination. To be valid, a feasibility study must be made by an outsider. Survey respondents will speak candidly, if at all, only to a professional outsider who establishes confidence and guarantees confidentiality.

Fortunately such feasibility study surveys have been found to be helpful to subsequent solicitation of contributions. Instead of raising suspicions and forearming, they tend to help the ultimate solicitation, to arouse and confirm interest in the purpose of the drive. People like to be asked for advice, so it is an act of cultivation when someone, especially an outside professional, raises the subject of a possible capital campaign and seeks a person's judgment on the matter.

Most contributions to capital drives will come from individuals. In your support constituency review for a capital campaign, you won't disregard corporations and foundations, but don't expect too much from them.

Organizational Readiness

Capital campaigns are demanding on board, executive, and development staff. Responsibilities need to be shouldered, critical decisions made, thorough long-range plans undertaken; a compelling case statement must be formulated, an organization put in place, and representatives selected to go out and ask for contributions.

Success depends on the campaign being led by people of stature, people recognized in the community and committed to the organization. The board supplies or secures that leadership. More than on anything else, success or failure hinges on board leadership—the strength, involvement, and participation of its members. In evaluating the readiness of an organization to move into a capital campaign, the strength of the board will count most.

Recruiting people to take part in campaigns demands all the care and attention you would give to soliciting a major capital gift

itself. *It is harder to get people to ask than to get them to give.*
Leaders ask and get others to ask.

Development staff, too, must be adequate for a capital campaign. The workload must be recognized and prepared for by personnel expansion and training. In major campaigns, outside professional assistance may be needed for implementation tasks as well as for guidance.

Capital drives require campaign organization, particularly as volunteers are a key feature. People work better in a structured environment where tasks are clearly limited and timetables are realistic. Available courses and manuals describe techniques and systems for organizing volunteers, not unlike those for a political campaign.

Campaign Plan

When an organization undertakes a formidable challenge such as a capital drive, it needs a comprehensive plan, particularly with a timeline schedule for completion of tasks, for each of the following elements:

- Analysis of funding needs
- Preparation of a case statement
- Installation of files, records, acknowledgment, and recognition procedures
- Prospect selection, research, and evaluation
- Cultivation of prospects
- Public relations, promotion materials, and special events
- Mounting and training a volunteer organization
- Asking for the major, "advance," donations.
- Asking every prospect.

Some organizations are ready for the challenge of a major capital drive, are equipped for it; others are not. It helps to bring in professional counsel. The big Harvards and Stanfords do. The small community service organizations and churches do. The criticality, and the need to be on the right track from the start, all point to the advisability of using professional help.

Counsel will work closely with board members whose participation is quintessentially requisite to success. Through a feasibility study, professional counsel can assure that the soundest decisions are made on these key matters: evaluation of *potential*—responsible advice as to whether or not a campaign can succeed and recommendation on a realistic goal; assessment of *readiness* of the organization to carry out such a major undertaking; and preparation of a *plan* incorporating all elements essential to a campaign strategy.

What does a feasibility study cost? Of course costs vary from those charged a national organization, a major university, or a hospital to those charged a small community organization. Today (1990), a thorough capital campaign feasibility study for a modest community organization will cost, at barest minimum, $12,000, and probably at least $15,000; for a major institution fees will be three or four times those amounts. Fees vary with the number of survey interviews deemed necessary for a reliable assessment of the potential. Expenses, too, including travel, will need to be reimbursed.

Once on the way with a campaign, organizations retain counsel to assist in the implementation of the feasibility study results they have adopted. Counsel works with staff and board members in carrying out the plan and offering guidance in the execution of campaign strategy. Currently, fees for this type of consultation run in the order of $800 to $1,000 per day. Perhaps a day or half-day every week or two weeks will be needed, with varying intensity as the campaign progresses and needs arise.

Organizations can and do retain counsel to manage campaigns, in addition to advising. Counsel gives on-site direction, drafts documents, and organizes the preparation and execution of the campaign—does everything short of actual solicitation. Such a management role assures professional expertise in the day-to-day operation of the campaign but is proportionately expensive because of the time commitment. For this type of assistance, counsel virtually adds a key person to the staff at consulting fee costs.

Nonprofit organizations, small and large, have an understandable reluctance to call in what they see as expensive outsiders to tell them about their own organization and its support constituency. But boards must realize that not only does the raising of capital funds differ from raising day-to-day operating and program money but also that it takes a trained outsider to assemble the underlying information on potential and an objective evaluation of readiness—factors that determine the success or failure of the campaign. In short, capital campaign stakes are high enough to justify going the added distance to fortify the commitment and reduce the risks.

An organization planning to retain counsel should invite written proposals, specifying the following matters to be covered:

- The nature and scope of the study, including the survey to be undertaken and the number of interviews to be held
- The content of the report to be submitted (presumably to include a complete strategy plan)
- The time required to do the study
- The cost of the study, with all attendant expenses.
- The person who will carry out the study

It isn't good enough to negotiate with a senior executive and then find a junior with a big title actually doing the job; the person to be assigned should be interviewed.

If there is one aspect of fund raising that more than any other should engage the full participation of the board, it is a capital campaign. You can take it as a certainty that a capital campaign will get nowhere unless the entire board is fully involved in every aspect of the effort—the planning, the giving, the asking.

17. Planned Giving and Bequests

For most trustees, planned giving is one of those confusing matters they would prefer to leave to others. Although they don't need to get enmeshed in the detailed technicalities, board members should understand the broad lines of planned giving in order to judge prudently when their organization should get involved.

All major gifts to nonprofit institutions are planned in the sense that they are carefully thought through; what has come to be known as *planned giving* is that category of gift made with a present commitment to a donation that the recipient institution may receive only after a period of time, often many years.

Nationally, the greatest portion of institutional gift income today, outside capital campaigns, comes through planned giving. It will apparently increase: Under the 1986 Tax Reform Act, nonprofit organizations are able to offer prospective donors various trusts and agreements that insurance companies, brokerage firms, and other profit-making organizations no longer can.

Three features characterize most planned giving:

- *It is a deferred gift.* As indicated above, planned giving involves a contribution that will not go to the recipient organization for a period of time after the commitment is made.
- *Such a gift comes from the donor's capital holdings*—real property, insurance, or securities—not from current income.
- *Donors themselves gain,* even as they help the receiving organization, often by a lifetime income above what they currently receive, as well as by tax benefits. This is an important consideration.

Note that a donation and delivery of securities or real property without any financial benefit to the donor other than tax deduction is considered an outright gift and, no matter how valuable the property and how carefully it has been arranged, it is *not* considered planned giving.

Because of the special characteristics, planned gifts are inextricably linked to estate planning. Even as donors should have their lawyers or accountants participate in arranging planned gifts, it is in the interests of the receiving organization to have the donor's advisers involved to assure that the transaction is in order and fully conforms to the donor's wishes.

Planned gifts fall into the following categories:

- *Bequests*: designating an institution as a beneficiary in a will
- *Insurance*: taking out policies with the purpose of making a contribution, or donating policies after their protection features are no longer needed (insurance is separately discussed in Section Eighteen).

- *Gifts of property or other assets*: contributing gifts through trust or other arrangements so that receipt of the gift is deferred to a future date while the donor and perhaps a beneficiary either have use of the property or receive its income
- *Gifts of income*: placing assets in trust for a period of years for the income benefit of the recipient organization, with the assets ultimately returning to the donor or a beneficiary

Lawyers explain a fundamental principle underlying most planned giving: Property consists of two interests, an *income interest*—its value as an income-earning asset—and a *remainder interest*—the ultimate ownership of the asset. Planned gifts involve the donation of one or the other of these interests; to contribute both income and remainder interest is to make an outright, not a planned, gift.

Remainder interest gifts are made by using

- A *Charitable Remainder Trust,* where a donor makes an irrevocable gift of appreciated property and receives in return each year either a fixed amount of income (Annuity Trust) or a fixed percentage of the market value of the property (Unitrust)
- A *Pooled Income Fund,* where, as in a mutual fund, the gift is combined with others into a common investment fund earning dividends and interest
- A *Charitable Gift Annuity,* a contract rather than a trust, whereby the donor receives a fixed annual income for life

An income interest gift in property is most often made by means of a *Charitable Lead Trust,* where, for the lifetime of the trust, the income goes to the institution, after which the assets revert to the donor or a beneficiary. A Lead Trust can be an enormously valuable gift: The donor in effect "lends" a large sum of money to an institution so that the institution receives its income during the life of the trust—possibly accumulating as much as the value of the "loaned capital" itself—after which the capital reverts to the donor or the donor's beneficiary.

Because of these special aspects, particularly the fact that the full benefit of the gifts may not be received for many years and that the donation is so closely tied to the donor's estate planning, institutions must manage a planned giving program quite separately from the solicitation of individuals either for annual giving or for capital campaigns. However, because the key prospects for planned giving will be identified through the research and cultivation of annual and capital supporters, a planned giving program must be closely coordinated with both annual and capital giving programs.

Planned Giving Programs

Charitable organizations tend to be reluctant to embark on planned giving programs, either because of their complexity or because of the deferred nature of the contributions; such programs produce little for current financial needs. Younger, smaller institutions may see themselves at a disadvantage competing in the planned giving field, but they need not be totally excluded. Donors committing an important share of their assets to an organization, and relying on that organization to produce income for them for the rest of their lives, may tend to look to large, well-established institutions such as universities and hospitals. However, small organizations can mount responsible planned giving programs, often on a shared basis with other institutions.

For large or small organizations, planned giving homework and preparation are necessary:

- A development staff or person must become knowledgeable in the ramifications of planned giving, usually through attendance at seminars. Except in large institutions where planned giving specialists can be retained, staff need not be expert, just knowledgeable. Outside counsel is available to guide the start-up of such programs.
- Legal assistance will be required to develop the mechanics of the program; to establish a Pooled Income Fund; to set up vehicles for administering annuities, unitrusts, and annuity trusts; or to draft suggested wording for bequests.
- Trustees have to understand and make a firm commitment to the program, recognizing as they do so that many years may pass before substantial income is received. Starting such a program

is making a long-term investment in the organization. Ideally, members of the board will create their own planned gifts in advance of announcing the program, even though their commitment may be no more than an addition to a will.

- Publications must be prepared describing various forms of planned giving and summarizing the advantages each offers. Although such printed materials are a necessary part of a planned giving program, they can readily be drawn up from those of other institutions because options and illustrations explaining them tend to be fairly standard.

The success of a planned giving program centers on the ability of the organization, its development staff, and volunteer board members to identify among the supporters and prospective supporters those few who, by the circumstances of their financial position, might benefit from a planned giving arrangement. Requisite circumstances are ownership in tracts of land, closely held companies, art objects, or other assets susceptible to capital gains tax if sold. Such donor prospects must be carefully cultivated over time. In the end, lawyers or accountants for both parties need to negotiate mutually beneficial arrangements.

Thus trustees of an organization considering mounting a planned giving program must ask themselves some tough questions. Has the organization reached a level of maturity so that it is seen as "here to stay," to be still around in twenty, thirty, or more years? Does the organization have a support constituency that includes people sufficiently close to it that at least some might be interested in associating their financial future with it? Does the organization have, or could it develop, staff or volunteer people to identify and approach prospects for planned giving arrangements? Does the organization have a board of trustees sufficiently committed to undertake the planned giving effort?

Steps to Get Started

To mount a planned giving program, the following actions, roughly in order, need to be undertaken:

1. *Prepare a plan.* Outline in some detail the planned giving vehicles; the organization of staff, volunteers, and outsiders; the timeline; and the costs.

2. *Secure approval of the board.* The board must be thoroughly briefed on the plan, give it full approval, and understand that appropriate member participation in the project will be expected.

3. *Prepare prototype instruments.* Draw up quite specific, "boilerplate" documents for each instrument to be used. They become the basis for discussion with a prospective donor's legal or accountant counsel; for example, draft clauses for wills, Charitable Remainder Trust instruments (both Annuity and Unitrust), stock powers, Pooled Income Fund Transfer agreements, and Charitable Gift Annuity contracts.

4. *Fulfill legal requirements.* Register planned giving vehicles with state or local offices; follow required IRS rulings; comply with state insurance laws.

5. *Prepare printed materials.* Prepare easy-to-read pamphlets or brochures to set out the alternative planned giving vehicles available, outline the advantages of each, and give clear, understandable examples. It is preferable to have a separate pamphlet for each vehicle. Patterns set by experienced institutions can be followed.

6. *Organize and train volunteer solicitors.* Form, organize, and train a cadre of planned giving specialists from staff, board members, and other volunteers—those who will select and solicit donors within the organization's support constituency.

7. *Identify the prospects; plan the solicitations.* The cadre of staff and board members will need to review and research the lists to identify likely prospects for planned giving, just as in selecting prospects for other major gifts. Incorporate general invitations to discuss planned giving opportunities in newsletters and other publications. Plan with care the actual approach to the prospect: *who* will make the approach? *how?* (letter? visit?)? With *what* suggested proposal? Cultivation and preliminary discussions follow the making of these decisions.

8. *Negotiate the gift.* The process of completing the transaction involves legal counsel representing both parties; occasionally

an organization will retain a professional planned giving counsel to close the deal.

Organizations are likely to delay moving forward on planned giving programs in order not to dilute efforts to raise money for current needs. It is true that planned gifts are generally for capital needs, but some forms yield current dollars. For example, the Charitable Lead Trust, where the donor gives immediate income, rather than deferred remainder interest; the Charitable Remainder Trust, where the donor, in addition to giving the remainder interest, gives a portion of the income interest to the charity; and gifts of life insurance, where the policy can be borrowed against or surrendered for its cash value.

Because a bequest is the simplest form of planned giving, an organization can begin without delay to encourage selected members of the support constituency to make provision for the organization in their wills. A postscript can be added to an appeal letter or a newsletter item can suggest such a bequest:

> Some members and friends of _____ have already included _____ in their estate plans. We hope you will consider this opportunity to make a major gift. Planned giving can be beneficial both to _____ and to your own tax and estate situation. If you wish to have more information on various options and benefits, please let us know at _____

A planned giving program will evolve, especially with smaller organizations, from the moment a single prospect emerges and negotiations are pursued. When others follow, the planned giving program takes shape.

It is up to the trustees to be alert to the possibilities of planned giving and not to let an opportunity be missed by negligence or timidity.

18. Life Insurance Contributions

Someone on your board is bound to say, "Why don't we use insurance as a fund-raising device?" Although in some circumstances for

some institutions seeking contributions through life insurance can
be an effective dimension of a development program, such programs are not without hazard and controversy. Their ramifications
are not always clear.

Trustees should be mindful of some basic truths about insurance giving. They should be aware of a distinction between the
contribution of *mature policies* and the taking out of *new insurance*
for planned giving purposes.

The assignment of ownership of a mature paid-up policy by
someone who no longer has need of its protective features can only
be welcome and encouraged. An institution can invite the donation
of such matured policies without preparation or program. Making
a life insurance gift is in fact simpler than making a residual gift
through a bequest and, from the standpoint of the receiving institution, it has advantages that a bequest does not have. Paid-up
policies already yield an income, have an immediate cash value,
and, unlike new policies, permit their donor a higher tax deduction.

For many of the millions of life insurance holders, their
beneficiaries have become self-sufficient or have died, their businesses have been sold, children educated, and mortgages paid, and
family protection is no longer a financial requirement. These policies are ripe for a planned giving program.

When considering selling *new life insurance* as a planned
giving technique, however, trustees should know about the following features:

1. In fund-raising terms, the basic purpose of life insurance
is the *creation of an asset* rather than the *transfer* of an existing
asset. Gifts of accumulated wealth—existing assets—are a luxury
available to the relatively few of great affluence: Those who donate
property of value make bequests of lifetime income, planned giving
gifts. Those, on the other hand, who buy insurance as a vehicle of
giving are creating an asset by making gifts from *current earnings,*
which will in time build an endowment.

2. Life insurance programs offer the donor an affordable way
to gratify a desire and get full recognition for a major gift by making an annual contribution for a limited number of years that is
only slightly greater than their customary annual gift. From the
donor's point of view, payments are made directly to the institution

and are fully tax deductible; they equate to and in fact become the premiums on the insurance policies. From the recipient's perspective, the institution becomes the owner and irrevocable beneficiary of the policy. Dividends or other accruals from the premiums come to the institution as immediate cash.

3. Insurance arrangements are available that allow the program to offer, and the purchaser to select, options depending on the interaction of such variables as age, health, and the size and length of the policy. In essence, while a portion of the premium covers the cost of protection, the bulk of it accumulates at interest to reduce the number of payments. The usual insurance-giving opportunities call for the donor's pledge of five or ten years' premium payments permitting the policy to sustain itself later from interest earnings.

4. The best candidates for a new life insurance gift are between the ages of twenty-five and fifty; they are successful professionals or business people with high incomes yet with limited or confined capital assets. Such people can, through an insurance program, make a major capital donation with a few manageable annual payments.

Two examples will illustrate:

- A twenty-year-old nonsmoking female creates a $50,000 endowment gift by seven annual payments of approximately $200 which, with its deductibility, could bring the ultimate cost to below $1,000.
- A forty-year-old male nonsmoker (who may regularly donate $100 to the annual fund) makes a $50,000 endowment gift by paying somewhat under $1,000 a year for eight years. For each of the first five years, a quarter of the annual premium goes to the institution as cash, serving as the donor's annual gift. When the tax deduction is calculated, the ultimate cost of the $50,000 deferred endowment gift could be as little as $5,000.

5. Arrangements are available for groups of individuals, such as a reunion class or a board of trustees, to purchase group policies for a single significant endowment gift. A group life policy usually requires at least twenty participants, all of whom pay premiums for, say, five years; upon completion of the payments, the

group receives full recognition even though the institution must wait to receive the funds.

The risks attending fund-raising life insurance programs must be squarely faced:

- The best insurance prospects are already annual giving donors. Soliciting these prospects can jeopardize the annual giving unless it is made clear that the insurance is to be a capital gift on top of the annual contribution.
- Prospects for insurance may be capable of making a substantial cash or securities donation for current use.
- An insurance program calls for a major administration and paperwork load. The development staff may not be equipped to handle the burdens of initial screening, solicitation, and monthly or other periodic billing for premium payments. The alternative of retaining an outside insurance agency for this relationship with important supporters can be dangerous. What happens, for instance, if premium payments stop?
- Insurance policy terms are based on interest projections. If interest rates fall, the policy doesn't pay up as soon as originally projected, to the consequent dismay of both donor and receiving organization.
- The institution should fully control the insurance program so that all contacts with donors are from the institution, not the insurance company. To turn over prospect lists to a commercial company, or to allow insurance salespersons to sell the policies, almost surely would be a mistake.

Insurance programs call for special techniques. Although they are designed to raise endowment capital, they are based on contributions of current income, not of accumulated wealth. Although the most likely prospects will emerge from the annual giving lists (where a letter appeal is useful as an introduction to their availability) or will be part of a group promotion, face-to-face discussion will be needed to complete the arrangements.

Leaving aside donations of mature policies, which are largely risk free, insurance programs can be effective only when there are large numbers of prospects particularly appropriate for insurance. In these circumstances, with careful planning and an eyes-open commitment by the board, an insurance program developed with the help of insurance professionals can prove a useful further dimension to a development program. But, as in all fund-raising, board members must closely oversee any commitment.

6

Asking:
The Board Member's Challenge

The essence of raising money lies in the relationship of an organization to its support constituency. A development program must concern itself with how it deals with its supporters, be they companies or individuals, large givers or small, as well as how it goes about asking for support.

Look at it this way. The interrelation of an organization with its supporters is a progression: first an awareness, then a familiarity and emerging interest, in turn an involvement, all leading to a contribution. In fund-raising terms, the progression translates itself into a series of activities: *public and community relations,* including visual and printed materials to attract the first awareness, followed by *cultivation* to develop the interest and invite involvement.

The contribution comes with an *asking,* for which there must be *research and preparation* and often *proposal writing.*

Board members need to be aware of all these activities. In some they can be helpful; in a few their participation is essential.

In this progression of activities, two elements are critical: the *case* to be made and the manner of *communication.* Before exploring the several activities, a word about these underlying elements.

Take first the case. Recall that people—and that means corporations and foundations as well as individuals—give money "to make a change for the good." From the start, your publicity, publications, cultivation activity, and solicitations must emphasize the core message of your case: what is needed in the community, in the nation, in the world; what is missing that calls for action, for change, for what it is your organization is doing. Everything you do or say in your publicity and printed materials should focus on the *why* of its existence, over and over. What is the problem "out there" that your institution is in business to improve? The temptation to talk and write about the organization itself, its history, activities, and needs, must be firmly resisted. The case points up the opportunity to support.

Trustees, in paying attention to public and community relations, cultivating prospective supporters, and participating in actual solicitations, will be of the greatest help if they keep their eye on the most compelling case to be made for supporting their organization.

Turn then to the element of communication. Although the concept of communication as the wellspring of all organizational activities is timeworn, it has validity. Every step in the progression of relationships with contributors—initial awareness, increased knowledge and involvement, solicitation, and proposal writing—depends on how effectively an organization communicates with its support constituencies—prospective, current, and regular.

Something can be learned of the value in different forms of communicating. Examine Exhibit 4, Ladder of Effective Communication.

The principle to be drawn from the ladder is that in every

Exhibit 4. Ladder of Effective Communication.

—face-to-face conversation
—small-group discussion
—telephone conversation
—handwritten letter
—typewritten personal letter
—large-group discussion
—videotape
—mass-produced letter
—newsletter
—brochure
—news item
—advertisement

aspect of fund raising you must strive for the highest level. Whether you are trying to interest a single person or a whole community of people, you better your chance of success at each higher rung of the communication ladder.

Put it to the test. If you want to introduce your organization and stimulate a beginning interest, a videotape is better than a written brochure, and a direct discussion is better than a video. If you seek to cultivate prospective contributors—individuals or institutions—your success will be far greater in a small, rather than a larger group. A direct discussion is more effective than a letter no matter how personal and persuasive the letter may be.

Clearly you cannot reach every member of a large organization, every alumnus, every annual supporter with a one-on-one conversation, but you can pick the most effective communication medium reasonable and proper in the circumstances. You can resist settling for a method low on the ladder when a higher step is available to you.

This principle is especially valid when you come to the asking. For annual giving and membership dues you will need to write; when your asking letter is more direct, more personal, you improve your chances of receiving a generous contribution. When you are going for the big donation from an individual, however, nothing short of a one-on-one conversation can be considered. And when soliciting business support, try never to settle for a written solicitation no matter how well known the corporate official is to the signer of the letter.

In thanking a donor—be it an individual or an institution—think how much more effective a hand-written note is than a cold, form-letter acknowledgment.

Trustees will be overseeing and frequently participating in the fund-raising support activities of public relations, cultivation, and asking for donations. They must be ever mindful that a strong, well-articulated case and effective communication methods will make the difference between success and failure.

19. Publicity and Printed Visual Materials

Trustees of nonprofit organizations have difficulty keeping public relations in perspective. For one thing, it is not always clear what is meant by the term *public relations*. For another, public relations can itself be an important aspect of the program activities of the organization—attracting students, audiences, patients, clients—but have only a limited or indirect effect on fund raising. Trustees can also be misled into believing a strong public relations effort is all there is to raising money.

It is helpful to make a distinction between *publicity,* on the one hand, and *printed and visual materials* on the other. Both need to be dealt with in a development program.

Although raising the public profile of an organization through publicity is important in the long run to the success of a fund-raising effort, publicity alone, except in special circumstances, will not bring in contributions. The exceptions are in major national drives for disaster relief or in seeking support for an advocacy position. Otherwise, it is not sensible to think of mounting a publicity campaign for its impact on fund raising. Publicity, if it is to have a significant effect, is a long-term activity. When the organizational image needs to be changed, brightened, or sustained, that cannot be accomplished overnight, certainly not in time to make or break a fund-raising campaign.

Printed and visual materials have value for cultivation; they attract and sustain interest. When it comes to actual solicitations, however, printed materials are not particularly helpful; they may even be a distraction. The letter is the principal medium for seeking regular, annual, "small" contributions; a personal visit or formal proposal is always involved in soliciting major individual gifts or corporate and foundation grants.

Although catalogues for schools, season announcements for cultural institutions, pamphlets, brochures, and flyers are all useful for an organization's programs, their value for fund-raising cultivation is often overestimated. Clearly it is useful to have an attractive handout or enclosable flyer to introduce people to the institution and its programs. Except for capital campaigns, however, expensive brochures do little for the fund-raising effort.

The two most useful cultivation materials are *annual reports* and *videotapes*. Each warrants discussion.

Annual Reports

In a single, attractive, and authoritative document, an annual report can convey the information appropriate to inviting and holding the interest of prospective or loyal supporters. As they will be interested in different matters related to the organization, the annual report should

- Highlight the organization's programs and activities
- Summarize the financial picture
- Draw attention to the organization's leadership
- Recognize its principal supporters (Some institutions use the annual report solely as a medium of gift recognition; they focus the entire publication on lists of contributors. Though useful for some, this practice is not recommended for the usual nonprofit institution.)

The annual report can be enclosed in correspondence, be left in the course of a visit, or be made available to inquirers. Regular supporters can receive the report in a comprehensive mailing.

A brief essay by the chairperson on a particular aspect of the organization's mission can be an attractive feature added to an annual report. It should be a thoughtful, even provocative statement rather than a broad review of program activities; its purpose is to gain reader interest.

And annual reports need not be annual. They can be issued in alternate years, or be called by a title such as "Report on Activities"; they can be produced with pockets to hold updated information.

Annual reports can be large, glossy, and expensive, or small, plain, and inexpensive; clearly, extremes in either direction should be avoided. Pictures are an attractive option, as are multicolor printing, marginal quotations, sidebars, and other design features. Remember that the value of the production warrants a significant investment of care and money, although it must fit the budget and image of the organization.

Videotapes

Video is a powerful and versatile medium of communication. Standing in the middle of the "ladder of effective communication," a videotape showing can be more useful than a written message and can supplement or replace an oral presentation, especially for large groups. Videocassettes, however, are expensive to produce.

Videotapes, like printed materials, are useful for program purposes as well as for fund raising. Although for smaller organizations a single video can sometimes serve for both program and fund raising, it is important to select and define the audience before embarking on a video project. Larger organizations with staffs and equipment can produce a different videotape for each type of audience.

As a rule of thumb in producing video presentations, count on about $1,500 per minute of final tape, and a cassette of less than four or five minutes is hardly worth the effort and expense. Although the cost of preparing the tape may include a few hundred copies, each additional cassette will cost $5 to $10.

Here are some things to watch for:

1. *Beware of compromises.* It is hard to make a good video, yet it must be done well. A poor video will harm the cause.
2. *Define your purposes and audiences.* Why are you producing the video, and who will see it? Many an expensive video gathers dust within weeks of its gala premiere.
3. *Be ready for a process of many steps.* Each will have multiple decision points on quality and cost: research and script preparation, talent recruiting, special effects, season "shootings," editings, revisions, and retakes.
4. *Allow plenty of time.* Count on at least six months from inception to completion.
5. *Choose the producer carefully.* Get competitive proposals. View samples. Check references.

Go for a video if you can find the money, but watch your step.

20. Research and Preparation for Asking

It is proverbial that the success of fund raising is 90 percent in prospect identification, research, cultivation, and preparation, and 10 percent in the asking.

Although research and preparation will be different for each category of giving source—government agencies, corporations, foundations, other nonprofit organizations, and individuals—some elements are common to all categories. For any prospect you need to know enough to make sound judgments on these questions (some of which were mentioned earlier in connection with business donations—see Section Thirteen):

- Which prospects have the capability and the interest, present or potential, to warrant solicitation?
- Who is the right person to approach? Who controls the giving?
- Who is the right person in your organization to undertake the asking? Who commands the respect of the prospect?
- What activity of your organization would the prospect be most interested in supporting?
- How much should you ask for?

- Is the prospect "ready"? What cultivation is appropriate before solicitation?
- Where, when, and how should the prospect be solicited?

Rarely are the answers to these questions clear-cut. Research can reduce uncertainty.

For individual major donation prospects, other questions need to be asked:

- What relationship does, or might, the prospect have to your organization?
- What are the prospect's interests?
- What are the prospect's giving habits?
- What family does the prospect have? Who are the closest friends?
- What personality traits of the prospect should influence the manner of asking? What values are important?

Research reference sources for foundation and business prospects are discussed in Sections Twelve and Thirteen. For individuals there are few reference books (*Who's Who, Standard and Poor's*); answers can come only from discreet exploration with mutual friends and business acquaintances, press clippings, or your organization's own files.

Organizations mounting capital campaigns heavily dependent on individual giving use "evaluating sessions," meetings of loyal supporters, to "rate" prospects' capacity and interest. From such sessions, development offices can glean critical information to guide their prospect research, cultivation, and asking.

Some people object to such evaluation sessions; they see them as invasions of privacy and betrayals of friendship and confidences. Objectors need not be so sensitive; participants in those sessions share an affection for the organization and are willing, within the bounds of appropriateness, to contribute key information on a broad list of prospects.

If doubts arise about the importance of research and preparation for asking, remember this: The missed gift opportunity may never be recovered. Each donation, especially in a capital campaign, is critical; don't risk short-sporting, underestimating the importance of preparing. You may not get a second chance.

In all research of prospects, no better source of valuable information can be found than board members.

21. Cultivation of Prospects

Although publicity and promotional activities build the general climate of opinion about an organization, cultivation efforts focus directly on prospective contributors. You cannot expect to receive donations from people until they know about your organization; you should not ask people for contributions until they are ready. Getting them ready is called cultivation.

Past donors are the best prospects for further contributions. The habit of giving brings strong loyalty, but it needs constant nourishment. Large one-time gifts and bequests come from cultivating annual givers.

Donors, especially prospective large donors, want to feel a direct, personal involvement with an organization. Bringing that about is cultivation, too. Send them materials. Invite them to occasions. Ask them for advice. Get them to do favors on behalf of the organization. One professional has put it aptly "Major donors deserve and demand constant special treatment. If you deny them such treatment, you remove their primary incentives for giving. Major donors should be provided with a consistent communication program, emphasizing personal recognition of their contributions. . . . The feeling of being an insider, of having personal contact with organization leaders, provides powerful psychological satisfaction" (Dennis L. Meyer, 1987).

Thanking supporters for their contributions is an act of cultivation: People appreciate the recognition of their generosity and feel closer to the organization, which makes them more likely to give again and make a larger gift. Board members can be especially effective in expressing appreciation for donations by regularly sending notes to donors, making known as a trustee that they are aware of the gift—especially if they themselves made the solicitation. Some organizations arrange evenings where board members rotate in coming in to make telephone calls of appreciation.

In capital campaigns where cultivation of major gift prospects is so important, face-to-face contacts are needed. Written communications are not enough. Feasibility study surveys of the
support constituency, far from hurting the effort, have proven to be
stimulators of interest in the organization and its plans.

Because cultivation is such a personal matter, and because it
involves the donors and prospective donors of major gifts, board
members must do the work. Knowing who the prospects are and
how to reach them, and finding reasons to be in communication
with them, is the beginning of cultivation. Escorting them to
events, seeking their advice, asking their participation in program
projects, even in fund-raising projects—these are acts of cultivation
and it is trustees who can best accomplish them.

A special note on cultivation. Former board members, often forgot-
ten, can be important to an organization: They can continue to give
generously and help in evaluating and making introductions to key
prospects. Current board members should make sure the chief executive and development office communicate regularly, and individually, with former board members.

22. Asking: The Hurdles

Why is asking for money so forbidding? Board members who take
the trouble to analyze this reluctance will be effective in overcoming
it and will be able to assist others to become committed askers. Here
are three aspects that may help in the analysis: (1) Asking is only
one part of fund raising; it is the main part but by no means the
only way a person can participate in the process. (2) Asking takes
many forms depending on who is being asked; some forms are not,
in fact, the kind that torments. (3) Asking causes different torments
for different people.

Asking Is Only One Part of Fund Raising

A trustee can do many things to assist the fund-raising effort without actually asking anyone for money. This is not to say that board

members need not do the asking; rather it offers alternatives to those who say, "I'll do anything but fund raising."

Trustees as yet unwilling to do the asking can take part in long-range planning—the clarification of funding needs. They can help formulate a persuasive case statement. They can add names to the prospect list and assist in the evaluation of names on that list. They can be active in the cultivation process. They can accompany a principal asker, write notes to support a written appeal, or thank someone for a contribution. All these they can do in support of the fund-raising effort yet stay short of asking for money.

They will soon see that someone must ask, that people don't give until they are asked. Trustees who participate will one day accept that they are the ones most suited to ask some prospects— and they'll do it. When they meet with success, they will be off and running, but they must be led to that success.

Asking Takes Many Forms

The fund-raising process, and therefore the asking, varies when the prospect is not an individual; it varies, too, depending on the type of organization being solicited.

Government grants (Section Eleven) come in response to a written proposal, usually specifically invited by a request for proposal (RFP). The proposal is the asking. If personal contact is called for, staff program specialists become the solicitors. Board members rarely need to become involved.

Foundations (Section Twelve) make grants by responding to formal or informal proposals. Trustees sometimes make an introduction where they have a contact and help to draft the proposal; neither action can be considered "asking."

Companies (Section Thirteen) may make a donation following a visit arranged or participated in by a trustee. The company response, however, will be made to an invited written request. There is no personal asking after the initial discussion that led to the invitation to submit a proposal.

Other nonprofit organizations—religious, professional, trade, and civic associations of various kinds (Section Fourteen)—also respond to written appeals. Trustees or staff members may participate in discussions, not solicitations, in which programs are presented and defended, often to a large group.

Only in seeking *individual* support does a direct, personal solicitation arise. Annual appeals (Section Eight) call for an asking, sometimes in writing, sometimes in person. Major capital gifts (Section Sixteen) always call for a visit to a prospect and a direct asking. Trustees should become involved.

Asking Causes Different Torments for Different People

Put aside those reasons board members may use for not getting involved with fund raising because "their interests are only in the programs," or "it isn't their responsibility," or "they are too busy to get involved": Those excuses go to the matter of board responsibility, not to fund raising itself.

For those who shun the asking because they see it as "preying on friends," or "twisting arms," or "begging," let them learn what giving and asking is all about (Section Two). Turn the tables: Do they see their friends who ask them for contributions to worthy causes as begging or twisting arms?

Some volunteers, though they may not admit it, are unwilling to risk asking for a contribution for fear of being turned down. The asker may indeed be refused, but it should not be cause for embarrassment or shame. An asker will be positive, will try hard to get a gift, but must be ready for a no. Again, look from the other side: You do not scorn the person whose request you have turned down. They won't scorn you either.

Of course, some people take to selling—for that is what asking is—more naturally than others. They are more comfortable projecting themselves and their enthusiasm with others. Not everyone will be a "wizard fund raiser," but many can be more effective in asking than they allow themselves to accept. With a keen interest in the organization in which they have accepted a leadership position, they can find themselves quite naturally asking for support, offering someone the opportunity to help make a change for the good.

There is one hurdle affecting all but a few trustees of nonprofit organizations: *procrastination*. More askings are avoided, deferred, and compromised because of a designated asker postponing the task than because of any other factor. Procrastination is the curse of fund-raising programs.

Procrastination is a mechanism—conscious or subconscious—to cover for the deeply felt torment about asking. We all find reasons not to do what we don't like doing. Yet if the job of asking is to get done, each asker must get on with the assignment, must face up to the natural tendency to find something else to do first and defeat it.

Trustees, executive officers, and development staffs must recognize this hurdle and deal with it openly. A necessary first step is to assure a full understanding of this whole giving-asking process. Built-in deadlines, firm schedules, reporting sessions, and follow-up telephone calls are all devices to combat the human tendency to put off the asking.

23. Asking: A Scenario*

Successful asking for money in essence takes common sense and enthusiasm for the organization you want to help. Nobody can give you the sense or the enthusiasm, but there are a few tips you can keep in mind when you are on the point of asking—or, as the hard-nosed call it, "closing."

Although approaches to corporations, foundations, or individuals vary, all solicitations have some things in common. For example, even before you get to the point of asking, you will have done your research and developed a realistic plan. You will have done your best to prepare if:

- *You have the right prospect.* If you are dealing with a company or foundation, be sure to see the highest appropriate official. If you are seeking an individual donation, be sure to include the spouse or any family member who will help make the decision.
- *You have cultivated your prospect.* Presumably your institution

*A version of this section was previously published in *IQ, CASE Independent Quarterly,* Council on Support and Assistance to Education, Fall, 1985.

cultivates its prospects with mailings or invitations to attend events. You know that your prospect is as ready as possible.

- *You know the prospect's interests.* You know the giving record and you have thought carefully about which aspects of your institution might be of greatest interest.

- *You will see the prospect.* Don't rely on letters or phone calls. A fund-raising visit is not a casual meeting. With the help of someone close to the prospect, you have made an appointment to visit; you have arranged for an appropriate time and place. Someone is with you, if that will help—two is better than one; three may be ganging up. The best combination is a trustee and a well-informed member of the staff. Recognize and respect an element of formality in what you are doing; don't take it lightly.

- *You know the amount you will ask for.* Arriving at the right figure isn't easy; it takes research on past giving, discreet consultation with those who know the prospect, and a healthy guess at what is possible.

When you ask for a contribution, you are selling your institution and what it does. From the moment you walk in the door for your solicitation visit, like any salesperson, keep your eyes on four "birdies":

Birdie One: The purpose of the visit is to ask for money. Everything about the conversation should relate to that. Get to it in the most comfortable, purposeful way. But get to it! Don't find yourself saying goodbye without having popped the question. It is truly surprising how many solicitors never quite get around to the asking.

Birdie Two: Talk opportunities, not needs. Foundations, companies, and individuals give where they think their contributions will make a difference. They are not interested in how much money you say your institution needs. They want to know what their gift will permit you to do. Of course, in your own board meetings you must talk about needs, or even deficits and cutbacks. But stay away from these grim thoughts when you are asking a prospective supporter for a contribution.

Birdie Three: Stay sensitive to what your prospect is thinking while you are talking. Never mind what he or she *should* be thinking. What is really going through the mind while you make your case? Beware glazed eyes. Don't be mesmerized by the sound of your own voice and your well-rehearsed presentation. Keep the prospect's interest.

Birdie Four: Begin, be brief, be off. Don't race, but don't linger. Most people, especially business executives, respect others who are direct and to the point. Humor, charm, and personal interest are fine, but get on with your purpose and get out. Sometimes your prospect will want to go slowly and talk, but don't count on it. Don't fall for an invitation to be a bore.

If these birdies seem obvious, just remember that the streets are full of askers who reported that everything went just fine—but who in fact didn't quite get to the question, didn't ask for a specific amount, forgot the prospect's interests, pleaded desperate need, overstayed their welcome, and came away empty-handed.

Assume now that you are informed, enthusiastic, and sensitive, and that you have your eye on the birdies. How will the visit go? Expect the unexpected. Be ready for anything from unanticipated generosity to a flat *no* that contradicts your groundwork. No two solicitations will be the same, but here is a reasonable scenario.

Step 1: Open with pleasantries. Not the weather; weather-talk turns many people off. Start with something to do with the prospect, something he or she would like to talk about, even the view from the window. But don't let this be too long. Remember Birdie One.

Step 2: Get to the subject. An easy way to begin is to say "thanks for seeing me." Offer to say a few words about your institution: "Would it be helpful if I brought you up to date?" Even if the institution is well known, such an introduction will be welcome. Tailor the conversation to the prospect's interests, which may even lead to questions and discussion. But again, don't take too long.

Step 3: Get to the asking. Ask the prospect to consider giving a specific amount. This step needs some discussion. Some say you offend your prospects if you tell them what they can or should give. But to fail to mention an amount is to invite a far, far smaller gift than you might otherwise get. Always put your request in terms of an opportunity—Birdie Two—and suggest a specific donation. You are not declaring what the prospect *ought* to do; you are simply asking that your suggestion be considered.

You might say what others are doing (without naming names). Better still, you can point out that your institution hopes that "three or four (or ten) friends (or companies or foundations) will contribute at a certain (stated) level" and you would like the prospect to consider being among that group. No one would take offense at that approach; people are pleased to be so included.

Mention the figure you have in mind early in the conversation. Say it clearly, and *only once*. It will be remembered. Before hearing a response, move quickly to other points: a multiyear pledge, some special program, some form of planned giving, public recognition of the donation. The amount you brought up will come up again, but not from you. Don't worry, it was heard. The ball has been in the prospect's court from the moment you named the figure.

Naming the amount early in the conversation helps you avoid the difficult situation of an early offer to give a gift that is too small. If that happens, point out that you are not asking for a usual or token gift. This request is special; you are there to ask for full support commensurate with what the prospect can give. You might even say, "Don't give just as an obligation; you don't have to give at all. You can say no, but we hope. . . ."

Back to the scenario.

Step 4. Be ready for any of a number of negative responses. We all tend to react negatively at first. You may get a flat refusal; if so, there's nothing you can do about it. Don't worry; you can't win them all. Thank your prospect and leave, keeping the matter open, if you can.

The first response might be a complaint about your institution, some personal dislike. Deal with it as sympathetically as you can and offer to look into it. Actually, if the prospect's first response avoids addressing the specific amount you put on the table, it may be a good sign: It's under consideration, not out of the question.

Some initial negatives aren't necessarily refusals, for example, "You've got me in the wrong league." Again, deal with these negative responses as well as you can. Don't push. Don't argue. Don't retreat. Leave the request on the table. It's still his or her move.

Sometimes it helps to stress the importance of doing something *now,* or to point to what others are doing. Only if it becomes completely clear that your figure is unacceptable should you begin any retreat. Even then, suggest another specific amount; don't fall back on such a weak statement as "I hope you will give whatever you can." Rather, allow time for the prospect to think it out alone.

Step 5: Leave on a positive note. Keep the solicitation open—rarely do you get a commitment on the spot. For companies and foundations, you might end the discussion by offering to submit a written proposal. With individuals, ask if it would help if you sent a summarizing letter for them to think about.

If a prospect does make a pledge on the spot, express your thanks no matter how small the donation. Don't belabor the point after the decision is made, but resolve to come back next year with a different approach. It is usually both futile and ungrateful to try to argue the figure up.

There is one exception to this rule, but it is rare. When a major giver offers a minor amount, you can sometimes express appreciation without formally accepting the offer. Instead, point out the different character of the request and ask the giver to consider a larger contribution. It takes a practiced, confident fund raiser to do this successfully, but there are occasions, especially in capital campaign drives, when a wealthy prospect comes to see what the difference is.

Step 6: Follow-up. In every case, promptly follow up a solicitation with a note. At the minimum, a word of appreciation is appropriate. Use a follow-up letter to improve your presentation, if you can do it briefly. Either way, the note is a tactful reminder that the request is still open.

What does this mean for trustees? Some, of course, will never allow themselves to ask for money, but when they are willing, they find it is not so hard. People can be encouraged, can be shown, can be tutored. A simple workshop, a half-day briefing, or a board meeting devoted to "how to ask for a contribution" can do wonders for a hesitant board member. But the best kind of training is to accompany someone else who is doing the asking: You see how it is done; you find yourself involved.

Asking for a contribution can not only be easy, it can be enjoyable as well. Enthusiasm, careful planning, and a deliberate, sensitive presentation can make a successful approach. Remember, you are offering people the opportunity to do something they may want to do, something that will give them pleasure; you are not twisting an arm or begging for alms.

Keep your eye on the birdies: The purpose is to ask for a gift; talk opportunities, not needs; stay sensitive to what your prospect is thinking; and don't overstay.

7

Organization and Procedures: The Board's Oversight Role

In raising money for institutional support, as indeed in all aspects of the organization, a responsible board is quite helpless without its executive and professional staff. Boards select chief executives and look to them to manage the activities. Chief executives hire staff personnel; establish organizational relationships within the staff; and motivate, direct, and supervise staff members. Chief executives see that all program activities, and the procedures by which they are carried out, are run in accord with plans and policies established by the boards.

In universities and colleges, the president, as chief executive, is the principal fund raiser. Not infrequently this is the case in other organizations too: The chief executive officer does most of the solicitation of major donations. But not so in all. When it is not the case, the solicitation job must go to the board itself; it must not be allowed to descend through the echelons of staff.

In any case, to fulfill their fund-raising responsibility, boards must oversee the decisions and activities of chief executives and their staffs without themselves preempting staff responsibilities or doing the work that staff should do. Because fund raising calls for more direct, personal involvement and participation of trustees than do other aspects of an organization, this line between management and oversight becomes harder to draw.

It is essential for board members to understand sufficiently what is involved in staff matters, in order to be able to oversee *and* participate. To this end, trustees need to address a number of issues specific to fund raising:

- *Staff*: What development staff do you need?
- *Volunteers and training*: How do you marshal and train volunteer support for the fund-raising effort?
- *Office procedures*: What is needed in files, mailing lists, and so on?
- *Computers*: What, if any, automation is called for?
- *A development strategy*: How do you establish a plan and goals?
- *Costs*: What will the fund-raising effort cost?
- *Evaluation*: How do you judge the effectiveness of the development program?

These issues are dealt with in the following sections.

24. Development Staff

Because all nonprofit organizations have to raise money to sustain themselves, they must assign a portion of staff time to fund raising. Whether it is a fraction of the time of the director of a three-person community service organization or a full position added to a twenty-five–person development office of a university or hospital, fundamental decisions about staff need to be intelligently made.

Although the organization and recruitment of personnel is a management responsibility, trustees cannot remove themselves entirely from involvement in these difficult judgments; the fund-raising operation is too important to the institution. Moreover, because an effective development staff works closely with board members, it is essential that trustees understand what is involved in maintaining a development office.

A preliminary caution for board members on nomenclature: Avoid the term *fundraiser* when referring to a development staff person. It is a misnomer—wholly out of line with the functions of development officers; they do not directly raise money. Moreover, the term carries the erroneous implication that the person so designated holds the responsibility for raising money, a responsibility that must lie with the board, and, at staff level, with the chief executive. The term *fundraiser* is equally misleading when referring to a fund-raising counsel, an outsider brought in to advise on fund raising, not to raise money.

Although the duties of a fund-raising staff vary with different kinds and sizes of organization, fundamental staff functions are the same. Development officers, first and foremost, do *research*—endless, systematic, thorough research. They research government agencies, foundations, corporations, churches, other nonprofit organizations, and individuals. They write *proposals*. They draft *correspondence*. They arrange *cultivation* events. They maintain *files and record systems*. They generate *ideas*.

Only occasionally do development officers visit foundations, corporations, or other prospects, and then it is with the chief executive or a board member, who, in most organizations, does the asking. In some large institutions, such as universities and hospitals, the top development officer will personally solicit contributions, calling on foundations and corporations. But by and large, development officers initiate, prepare, point the way, assist, and accompany, but do not themselves do the asking.

Development officers, on the whole, are to be "heard but not seen"; they are the drones who do the work, prepare the materials and recommendations, and then send the chiefs in to see the prospects while they stay in the background. Staff work can be drudgery: critically important but endless. Although development officers must work comfortably with board members, as a rule they do not successfully replace board members or the chief executive in making the key visits to prospective supporters. They frequently have trouble adjusting to that limitation.

When looking at staff for fund raising, these are the questions that invariably arise: *size of staff, qualifications, recruiting sources,* and *pay.*

Size of Development Staff

As you hear time and again, it takes money to raise money. You also hear that the organization cannot afford an additional development position or even a person solely occupied in development tasks. Perhaps, however, the organization cannot afford *not* to have such a person.

Start with a clear understanding of what this person is to be hired to do. What is needed is not a job description but an identification of functions now inadequately performed and not assignable to others in the organization. It is easy to reach such an understanding in a large organization where the fund-raising duties can be broken down among the development staff: research, records, and mailing lists; annual giving, memberships, and program support; foundation and corporate support; capital campaign and planned giving. For a small organization where workloads are shared, however, it is more difficult to judge whether another position is needed and what precisely an added development person will do.

As a rule of thumb, with all the risks of such generalizations, it can be said that an organization with an annual budget of $300,000 probably needs at least one person giving half-time to the fund-raising program, especially if the budget is heavily dependent on contributed, rather than revenue, income. Organizations with annual budgets of more than $500,000, again depending somewhat on the degree of reliance on contributed rather than revenue income, probably need a full-time development officer. As a budget goes up, further assistants under a development officer are needed.

Qualifications and Experience

Although a track record—positive experience in fund raising—is desirable, personal qualities can be given higher priority in selecting development officers. Assuming the candidate already has such assets as integrity, willingness, and humor, the key personal qualities to look for in a development officer are

- *Initiative*: being a self-starter, someone with ideas and a willingness to risk moving with them
- *Communication*: an ability to write and speak effectively
- *Compatibility*: a capacity to get along with people—associates, board members, prospects
- *Humility*: a willingness to let others take the front position

These qualities, along with the simple ability to produce, to get out the work, are ones you can't teach or train; a person has them or doesn't. Look for them first and then look for the experience and skills you believe the position calls for.

Every organization would like to find, at a salary level it can sustain, a person with these qualities who also has experience in fund-raising techniques. Often, however, it is preferable to take on a strong junior person who can learn the skills on the job than to choose expensive experience when the key qualities are in doubt.

Sources of Recruitment of Fund-Raising Staff

Good, experienced development officers are hard to find. There are not enough of them to satisfy the demand. As a result, development officer salaries have risen sharply; many young and inexperienced people have been attracted into the field and there is widespread job shifting.

A recent survey of college and university fund-raising personnel (Pocock, 1989) found that more than half of those questioned had had no more than two years of experience. One in five said they were looking for a new job for higher pay, or they were dissatisfied with what they saw as unrealistic expectations imposed on them from above.

Organizations seeking to fill a development position can themselves advertise for and screen applicants or they can retain a search firm to seek out qualified candidates. The former course is usual because it is less expensive. Philanthropy and fund-raising journals, as well as local papers, carry job opportunity ads, and the usual procedures can be found in reviewing résumés, interviewing, and checking references.

Using a search consultant can be a sounder, though more costly, way to go. A search firm can ferret out reluctant or sleeper applicants, able people who have not considered moving because they are satisfied and doing a good job where they are. The best reference you can get is that an organization does not want to let your candidate go. By contrast, those responding to advertisements are either out of a job or want to move and you don't know why.

Getting the right person is worth a special effort and perhaps expense; what you save could be the months you would spend finding that your new employee is inadequate.

If you do use a search firm, be thorough about selecting one. Seek one that specializes in nonprofit institutions, preferably in your field. Get competitive bids; ask for precision on fees and timing; interview the representative who will handle your business. Check references as you would on an employee.

The role of a search consultant is quite different from that of a fund-raising counsel. Wholly different techniques and abilities are called upon for executive search. Do not assume that fundraising counsel will be able to, or should, undertake the search assignment.

Whether the candidate comes from advertising or through a search firm, it is as important to check references thoroughly for development positions as it is for any other. Check the key qualities as well as the record of experience. Find references other than those suggested by the applicant. Board members and known funding supporters of the organizations of previous employment are good possibilities.

A problem arises in evaluating these references: You can't confidently assign credit and blame in raising money. As President Kennedy was wont to say, success has many parents—failure is an orphan. If an organization has raised a lot of money, the chair, the chief executive, and the development officer are quick to claim credit; if the campaign has flopped, it is said that someone else didn't measure up. Evaluate the references as well as the applicant.

How Much to Pay

The salary to be paid the development officer inevitably presents a quandary. With proven development officers in such short supply, the market has in some cases raised their salaries above those of senior program officers, bringing about, quite naturally, personnel distress. If the organization's activities depend on its raising funds, and someone with proven experience is called for, it may be necessary to meet the market rate and deal forthrightly with the internal stress engendered.

Today you may be able to find for a relatively low salary a minimally experienced but clearly able person with the qualities you need. If you are so lucky, you must be ready to raise the salary promptly and often, because others will be ready to raid.

A salary guide drawn up by a technical group is shown as Exhibit 5. For schools, colleges, universities, and some other institutions, additional perquisite compensations are sometimes paid in the form of tuition assistance, housing assistance, cars, club memberships, and deferred income plans.

25. Volunteers and Training

We normally think of philanthropy as giving money, but it is also giving time and effort—volunteering. Volunteers come in many forms, and all assist nonprofit organizations by saving the cost of staff, often doing jobs a staff member cannot do. Board members are volunteers. Other volunteers help with programs: as teachers and docents; as coaches and "big brothers"; as hospital assistants and home care aids. Volunteers can be invaluable in fund raising.

Board members need to be concerned with what volunteers can do, how they are organized, and how they are trained.

What Volunteers Can Do

The major role that volunteers can play in capital campaigns is discussed in Chapter Five. Volunteers can help in other aspects of fund raising, as the following list shows.

- *Fund-raising events*: dreaming up, organizing, and managing in every detail the fund-raising events and benefits (a function that comes at the top of the list because volunteers are at once essential to it, are the best qualified for it, and make a great contribution by keeping paid staff from being diverted to it)
- *Office work*: maintaining mailing list, records, and files; envelope-stuffing; general staff assistance
- *Printed materials and newsletters*: assembling, processing, distributing
- *Gift shops*: clerking, managing
- *Public awareness*: receiving visitors, guiding, making speeches

Exhibit 5. Salaries: Directors of Development.

	Lowest	*Average*	*Highest*
By Budget Size			
Under $100,000	$19,500	$37,500	$49,000
$100,000 to 200,000	14,800	33,507	60,000
$200,000 to 500,000	15,015	27,444	60,000
$500,000 to 1 million	14,223	28,251	50,000
$1 million to 5 million	16,902	35,035	78,000
Over $5 million	15,870	43,776	94,000
By Location			
Metropolitan	$15,000	$36,675	$94,000
Other urban	14,223	33,085	65,000
Rural	16,902	30,815	78,000
By Region			
Northeast	$17,500	$38,537	$94,000
Southeast	16,902	35,046	82,000
Midwest	15,870	33,959	80,000
Mountain	14,223	30,377	69,000
Southwest	17,500	34,955	65,000
Pacific	18,708	36,531	74,000
All	$14,223	$35,155	$94,000

Source: 1989 National Nonprofit Wage and Benefit Survey, Technical Assistance Center, Denver, Colo., 1990.

Volunteer Organization

Small nonprofit organizations can achieve valuable widespread involvement in fund raising by having advisory committees and by appointing non-board member volunteers to committees. Large institutions—museums, symphonies, theaters, schools, colleges, and universities—usually need a formal organization of volunteers: volunteer councils, "friends of _____," associates. Each will have honorary officers and members as well as those volunteers committed to getting the job done.

Training for Fund Raising

A board must ensure that its fund-raising volunteers, as well as its own members, are trained in asking for contributions. With skilled personnel, this training can be accomplished internally, but generally outside help adds a dimension. A professional should be called in if the board is satisfied that his or her presentation will be tailored to the organization's needs.

Workshops, conferences, and training courses abound, geared for beginners or experts, for staff or volunteers, and ranging from three-day expensive affairs to modest two-hour sessions. They are valuable but can be overdone: conference congeniality may be more an attraction than education.

Some find role-playing a useful training technique. It's not easy: Even with skilled leaders, participants become self-conscious actors before their peers, which reduces the training value.

In any event, training does not solve all the problems of fund raising. As with learning any skill, we can be told what to do, we can watch it done well, but in the end we must do it ourselves if we are to master it. Volunteers, especially board members, should be encouraged to get started toward involvement by participation in all phases of fund raising—sitting in on the planning, joining in the preparation, and especially accompanying a solicitor as an observer. Such is the way to full involvement. Such is the way to personal success in raising money.

26. Office Procedures and Computers

Trustees ask, "Why should I get involved in office procedures and computers?" Fund raising can be seriously handicapped by inadequate office procedures; trustees need to be at least familiar enough with development office operations to understand staff needs and to make policy decisions. As for computers, although automation can be a boon to a nonprofit organization, it also presents complex problems that call for difficult and costly policy decisions. Board members can bring helpful experience to the table and can learn enough of the organization's computer needs to be more effective.

But there is a warning, too. When board members become directly involved with development office procedures and computer use, they are taking risks: Their role is one of oversight; they must guard against impinging on management's responsibility.

Office Procedures

As board members become involved in fund-raising activities, they need to become familiar with such procedural matters as *files, profiles, acknowledgments,* and *renewal routines,* which produce the papers and actions trustees will deal with.

Files. Start with an individual file folder on each major contributor and prospect. Entry into a computer data bank does not obviate the necessity for this individual file. Folders should be classified or color-coded to indicate an individual, a foundation, a corporation, or another nonprofit organization.

The key to successful filing is the inclusion of *all* information that even remotely relates to the prospect, the prospect's interests, and the prospect's potential. Files should carry formal reports, news clippings, correspondence, memoranda, and even snippets scribbled on paper.

Filing discipline is admittedly difficult to impose. All staff members and trustees *must* send to the development office copies of all correspondence and notes of conversations with prospective contributors, no matter how trivial they may seem at the time, and the development office *must* scrupulously file them. Too often organizations overlook the importance of such files; they assume someone will remember the details months or years later when the information suddenly becomes important because it is time to ask for the big gift. The problem of not having the information at hand when it is needed is far greater than the chore of maintaining good files.

Profiles. Board members and staffs are constantly reviewing lists of contributors and prospects in all categories. To make such reviews efficient, a separate profile sheet can be prepared on each prospect. Profile sheets, to be most useful, are on a single page with a form to show only key information: name, address, phone numbers, names of potential contacts, and a summary chronology of correspondence actions and past contributions.

Profile sheets are to be continuously updated and reproduced for sorting by category, geographic location, or other criteria; copies can be assembled ready for review by the chief executive, development committee, or development staff itself.

Acknowledgment and Renewal Routines. Every contribution deserves a prompt acknowledgment. The more personal the expression of appreciation, the better chance for another donation. For large contributions, several letters of appreciation are not too many. Everyone says "of course" to such procedures, but too often the routine is not established and "thank-yous" can be overlooked. Board members must see that they are not. It is surprising, for instance, how many organizations, quick to acknowledge an individual's gift, fail to thank a foundation or company. You want them to repeat, too.

Renewal dates must not be lost in the shuffle. It is important to choose or design a mechanism that fits the conditions of your organization and to follow it without fail.

Computers

These days, board members can be counted on to have a degree of sophistication about computer use. They don't need to be expert, but they surely should not be naive or antedeluvian about them. They need to know enough to apply what they know to the particular needs of their nonprofit organization.

Computers do present complex problems. All nonprofits are getting computers and word processors, upgrading their capabilities, spending a lot of money. Frequently they are not getting what they need. Although development office needs for automation often initiate computer deliberations, the needs of program management, administration, budgeting, and accounting should be considered in discussions of *needs assessment, software, hardware,* and the hiring of *consultants.*

Needs Assessment. Defining your computer needs, difficult as it is, is a healthy exercise: It forces staff to think through every step of daily operations, brings to the surface deeply submerged assumptions, and helps to resolve conflicting priorities. All staff members should be involved. Every detail needs to be made explicit if you are going to avoid expensive errors and make proper use of a major investment.

Clearly a computerized data bank and filing facility can be of enormous help to a large, and even a not-so-large, nonprofit organization. But sophisticated automation is not for all nonprofits. Establishing the margin between cost and benefit of automation depends on such variables as budget and development staff size, and particularly on the quantity of data to be handled. Some organizations need not undertake expensive computer installations; others make a serious mistake in failing to do so.

Software. Look into software needs before you even start talking hardware. Automation offers almost limitless capabilities (which is one of the problems). With *word processing,* automation capabilities for letters and proposals are so evident that to avoid them is to hide one's head in the sand. The effectiveness of spreadsheets, personalized letters, and desktop publishing constitutes a breakthrough that is hard to deny. Another advantage is *data management*: Lists, records, and resource controls are simplified for management of all programs. *Financial management* vastly reduces the burdens of calculation and presentation of budgets and accounts. But the computer can only do what is in the program, what it has been told to do. Someone must do the manual work properly or the computer is not a blessing or a timesaver.

For fund-raising purposes, automated data management can be of special assistance in three key operations:

- *Mailing lists* (discussed with Annual Appeals in Section Eight): Virtually unlimited numbers of names can be coded in various categories, kept current, and called up selectively for cultivation mailings, appeal letters, and invitations.
- *Records*: Summary information, such as giving records, can be maintained on contributions and prospects, readily available for reference or for prospect lists, "action books," and reports.
- *Appeal letters*: With word-processing capability, personalized letters can be produced for all annual appeals.

Experts debate whether you should buy ready-made fund-raising software or design your own; they marshal technical and personnel competence arguments on both sides. However, to create a custom software program can take endless time and result in an untested program. On balance, therefore, it would appear that, unless your computer-sophisticated personnel are also fully knowledgeable about development needs (rarely will computer experts admit they can't meet any needs), it pays to buy a software package, carefully checking references among other nonprofit buyers. From your organizational computer-needs assessment, you have the basis on which to prepare a software "request for proposal" inviting vendor bids.

Hardware. Select the hardware to fit the software. Nonprofit organizations usually find it preferable to lease, rather than buy, computer hardware. Hardware soon becomes obsolete; as with an automobile, you want to be able to trade frequently to get the new features.

Check carefully. For both software and hardware, be sure that your organization has looked into *warranties, installation, training, operating support,* and *upgrading of software.* Do more than check the vendor's references: Visit users, if you can, to see how they operate, what to watch out for.

Consultants. Computer consultants can be useful at each stage: helping to find and express in technical and precise terms the needs assessment—what automated procedures can do for you—and particularly in choosing software and hardware. Too many details related to automated fund-raising procedures escape even a knowledgeable staff person, and a vendor's advice is, of course, not disinterested, whereas a consultant makes a business of finding what will suit you.

When deliberating about computer consultants, beware of insiders bearing gifts. The computer expert loaned by a well-intentioned friend may know little about your organization or about fund raising. You may be on safer ground hiring an expert on contract.

27. A Development Strategy and Plan: Setting Goals

General Eisenhower, before he became president, spoke about the necessity for planning along these lines: You must plan even though the plans will rarely be followed and fulfilled; the exercise of planning is necessary to give purpose and direction to a program and organization.

Thorough and careful planning is as important for fund raising as for any other program or operation. Setting specific, realistic goals is especially important for fund raising because they serve as a stimulus for the organization to extend its efforts. Boards must insist on such planning both to determine that the direction the organization is going is deliberate and to establish bases for its own periodic review, assessment of progress, and approval.

A simple form works well for setting out a fund-raising plan or strategy—one that can also be useful for other programs. It combines two dimensions: First, separate each part of the overall strategy, the core elements, and then, for each element, lay out the components of the plan.

For a development program, the core elements are of three kinds:

(1)　plans for reaching out to each of the *sources of support*—what is the strategy for getting contributions from government, business, foundations, and other nonprofits, and the several ways of soliciting individual donations, including fund-raising events

(2)　plans for seeking support for special *projects*—what fund raising is directly related to special activities, such as exhibits, research projects, scholarship funds, and so on.

(3) plans for strengthening each of the development *activities*— what actions are planned to improve case statements, filing system, mailing list, annual report, planned giving, and so on.

Having identified all the elements to be involved in the strategic plan, turn to what you are going to say about each one. Think through the same five components for each of the elements of the plan, specifically

1. *Objective*: What broadly are you trying to achieve with the element of the program?
2. *Present situation*: Where do you stand now?
3. *Courses of action*: What steps do you plan to take?
4. *Goals*: What specific markers, dollars, or achievement points will you strive for on the way to the objective?
5. *Costs*: What will the plan for the element cost?

Stripped of unnecessary padding, a strategic plan for even the most extensive development program can be kept to twenty or twenty-five pages. As such it can give the development office a sense of purpose, and it can be the principal instrument of a development committee, giving the committee a clear focus and a basis of evaluation of performance (see Section 29). It can be revised annually for approval by the board.

28. The Costs of Fund Raising

Nonprofit boards should surely know how much their fund raising *costs*. They should also determine the method of making public *disclosure* of those costs.

Costs

Because the cost of raising money has so many variables, arriving at useful guidelines is difficult. Nonprofit institutions experience different cost levels in different locations, in different sizes and kinds of organizations, and in different degrees of maturity of their fund-raising programs. It is difficult to validate cost figures until a program has a minimum of three years of experience.

Each type of fund-raising program will have its own cost demand and structure: mass direct mail, annual giving, corporate and foundations solicitation, special events and benefits, capital campaigns, and planned giving.

A further complication arises when you arbitrarily allocate such indirect costs as rent, administration, and facilities to each institutional program. To recommend a single or simple formula, or even guideline, for estimating development program costs would therefore be misleading.

The National Society of Fund Raising Executives Committee on Public Education on the Cost of Fund Raising published a comprehensive review of the subject in their *Task Force Report* (Green-field, 1988). The following figures for cost estimates of different kinds of fund-raising programs are drawn from that report.

- *Mass direct mail.* Mass direct mail programs, as earlier discussed (Section Nine), are appropriate for few organizations. Since name acquisition is the principal reason for going to the expense of leasing lists, the potential value as regular givers of those who respond is the measure of whether the cost is warranted. The high cost of a first mailing—as much as $1.50 per dollar raised from a postulated 1 percent response—therefore cannot be the basis for deciding on the investment. The cost of the second and third mailing to those who responded to the first mailing is sharply reduced to perhaps 22 cents, or even less, for each dollar raised. For such later mailings there is no lease charge and the rate of return could rise to 50 percent.
- *Individual annual giving appeals.* Because annual mail appeals are made to members, past contributors, and likely prospects, the costs run far less than do mass direct mail costs. For a large mailing, the cost can be as low as 10 to 15 cents for each dollar response.
- *Corporate and foundation solicitation.* Although the full cost of preparation for each solicitation will be high, donations, once made, are higher than most individual contributions. The cost

per dollar raised therefore can be even lower than for individual annual giving appeals; as little as 7 to 10 cents per dollar raised is not out of the question.

- *Special events and benefits.* Events serve other purposes than fund raising, but they are expensive. A *net* cost of 50 cents for every dollar raised is not excessive, but board members must watch carefully to ensure that, with the enthusiasm and inexperience of volunteers, costs don't get out of control. Although cost figures can be cut down by donations of facilities, food, or entertainment, such donations should not be allowed to obscure real costs.
- *Capital campaigns.* Because capital campaigns have a limited time commitment, depend on volunteers, and bring in large donations, their cost per dollar raised is low. On the other hand, if professional fund-raising counsel is retained, especially as "resident managers," the expenses can be high. Costs per dollar raised will presumably be less with higher dollar goals. Five to 10 cents per dollar raised is reasonable, and 15 cents or even higher for each dollar raised is acceptable. That's $150 spent for each $1,000 raised.
- *Planned giving.* Much planning time and cultivation goes into each planned giving donation, but, as with other capital contributions, the gifts are large. In planned giving, 25 cents per dollar raised is arbitrarily considered a reasonable guideline, though, again, the cost per dollar raised goes sharply down with larger gifts.

A report on a survey of fund-raising performance of some 1,200 academic institutions, published by the Association of Governing Boards of Universities and Colleges (Pocock, 1989), reached some conclusions that may also apply to nonprofit institutions other than academic. The survey found, for example, that academic institutions with lower ratios of fund-raising costs to receipts shared these significant characteristics: They spent 4.1 percent of operating budgets on development, approximately one-third more than the average academic institution; they have larger fund-raising staffs; their higher costs are more than offset by higher receipts; and they spend 14 cents for every dollar raised, compared with 22 cents for all other academic institutions.

The development office is one of the few programs of nonprofit organizations that "pays for itself." This alone suggests that budget allocation to fund raising is an investment, but how big that investment should be is a difficult judgment to make. An organization can approximate its fund-raising allocation by applying an average cost-per-dollar-raised figure of 20 cents to the estimated total of contributions needed. In other words, start with a rough estimate of development costs running, over a reasonable period of time, at one-fifth of contributed receipts. Then refine that ballpark figure by closer examination of probable cost for dollar raised of each development program in the total fund-raising effort.

"Bottom-line" strategists on the board may be unhappy that managers cannot come up with a definitive cost figure as for other programs, but in fund raising, neither costs nor results can be readily pinned down.

Disclosure

Corporate and foundation officials in particular expect their donations to go to the charitable purpose and not to administrative or fund-raising costs. They may ask for figures on fund-raising costs to confirm that expectation. Responsible organizations must be in a position to respond openly.

Government regulation on disclosure has intensified recently, in part stimulated by alleged Iran-Contra and religious broadcast misuse of donated funds. Many states now require annual registration and prescribed financial reports to be made available on request.

The Internal Revenue Service has its form 990, which all charitable organizations (except churches) with gross receipts of more than $25,000 must file. These forms are available to the public most readily at the Foundation Center libraries.

Whether as a response to government regulation or of their own accord, boards of responsible nonprofit organizations should make available full financial statements disclosing assets, liabilities, fund balances, revenues, and expenses. Expenses should be broken down to show costs of program services, general management and administration, and fund raising.

29. Program Evaluation

Boards, just as managing executives of nonprofit organizations, are constantly plagued by the knotty problem of determining what they can reasonably expect from the fund-raising program. As a key part of their oversight responsibility, trustees must know if the development program is performing as it should, is effective, is meeting realistic goals. But the variables that go into success in raising money are so many and so hard to judge, they can frustrate a board.

Some boards, troubled with the way things are going with the fund raising, want to check up through an evaluation and make immediate changes. Confident and satisfied boards, on the other hand, want evaluations, as do leaders of efficient business companies, for constant review and exposure to new ideas. Boards, too, can be uncertain, often with good reason, about their own leadership of the development program and want guidance.

One often hears the saying, "if it ain't broke, don't fix it." The better advice would be not to wait for a crisis to make a change; adjustments big and small come a lot easier when not made in a pinch. Program evaluations can lead the way to evolutionary change.

But the evaluation process for development programs is not easy. At a minimum, boards and development committees working with development staffs can examine the elements of the fund-raising program one by one and look for ways to strengthen each. The table of contents of this book offers an outline to assist such a review.

The comprehensive development strategy plan discussed in Section Twenty-Seven can also serve as a means of self-evaluation: A review of the planned courses of action and goals for each element of the program can give an overall picture of program performance.

These self-evaluations should be at least annual. While they are necessary and helpful, they may not be fully satisfactory. Each organization is different: its mission, its age, its reputation in the community, the loyalty of its supporters, its competitive position, its organizational strengths. All these features that materially affect the ability to raise money are extremely difficult to evaluate, especially if an organization judges itself.

For the most useful assessments you need objectivity and a thorough knowledge of the fund-raising field—something more than an intimate familiarity with the organization's own program activity. Because personalities are involved, evaluations are always sensitive. Moreover it is all but impossible to perform a self-assessment while carrying on the program. For these reasons self-evaluations can be awkward.

Nor is it usually helpful to bring in peers from like organizations to pass judgments on colleagues: The same questions of detachment and limit of new perspectives arise.

Although it calls for a larger commitment, an alternative course is to bring in an outside fund-raising consultant, if the timing is propitious, to make a *development audit*. (See Section Thirty-One.) Such an audit is not to be confused with a feasibility study, which is an external examination of an organization's constituency in order to assess the potential for attracting capital donations. An audit is internal, focusing on the effectiveness of the various components of the program. It involves a review of the entire fund-raising effort—the mission and funding needs, the case, the appeal to the various elements of the support constituency, the organization, personnel, procedures, and budgets. Board leadership and participation in fund-raising come under scrutiny. The outcome is a comprehensive analysis with recommendations—a blueprint for moving forward.

An audit is appropriate in times of trouble and uncertainty, or to reinforce a successful program. It can precede a feasibility study, anticipate a capital campaign, check on whether the organization is ready to embark on such a venture. Audit evaluations can also be useful in times of personnel turnover: A realistic review of objectives and expectations, and an inventory of assets, can provide a strong foundation for transition to new leadership.

Boards, closely advised by executive officers, should make deliberate plans for periodic evaluations of development programs. In no other way can they have confidence in the financial health of the organization. Experience shows that competent executive directors and development staffs welcome rather than fear program evaluations, including professional audits; they are confident an objective assessment will confirm their present practices and point the way to new opportunities.

8

Special Concerns
for Board Involvement

30. Cause-Related Marketing
31. Professionalism, Ethics, and Regulation
32. Using Consultants

30. Cause-Related Marketing

If the subject of "cause-related marketing" enters the picture of a nonprofit organization, the board should know it and make the decisions. It is a policy matter and it is controversial.

Maurice G. Gurin, chairman of the American Association of Fund-Raising Counsel's Trust for Philanthropy, has defined cause-related marketing in these terms: "[A] company obtaining an exclusive license to link its product or sales with a voluntary organization's cause, promotes that linkage to increase its sales, and allocates a portion of the funds thus generated to the organization" (Gurin,

1989). He has called cause-related marketing "the most serious current threat to fund raising for nonprofit causes."

Cause-related marketing is best illustrated by an early and certainly prominent example. In 1983 the American Express Co. offered the Statue of Liberty Foundation, as part of its major restoration campaign, a dollar for every new American Express card application and a penny for every time its charge plate was used. The American Express Company and the Statue of Liberty authorities, in a major and prolonged promotion featuring the arrangement, led the public to believe the funds generated were "contributions" to the Statue of Liberty restoration. In fact, though $1.7 million went to the campaign, none was a contribution: For American Express it was a business expense toward a company profit; for the individual it was a purchase.

Other prominent examples of cause-related marketing include Coca-Cola and "Hands Across America," and Philip Morris teaming with the U.S. Government Archives to promote the Bill of Rights.

Cause-related marketing is *business* marketing, not marketing of a nonprofit organization. The controversy is not a question of whether it is sound business but rather, whether it is sound philanthropy. If it brings in money to a charitable organization, it certainly is attractive. But is it, or can it be, harmful to the nonprofit organization? Is cause-related marketing an unwelcome business intrusion into the philanthropic sector?

Consider the following aspects:

- Companies, in making cause-related marketing arrangements, are looking at the potential for market exploitation, not at the social values. They are giving away nothing; they are gaining.
- Consumers responding to such marketing devices may be misled into thinking they are "giving," when in fact they are buying.
- If companies use such marketing devices as a substitute for philanthropy, it is clearly a detriment to nonprofit organizations generally.
- If companies other than the one with a market-related promotion become reluctant to give to an organization identified with

such a profit-making arrangement, the fund-raising program of the receiving company may be hurt.

• The temptation will be present for a nonprofit recipient to modify its program to suit the wishes of the company whose profits they are sharing.

Those who favor cause-related marketing say with reason that philanthropic organizations gain, perhaps greatly, from such arrangements. Although it may not be a contribution in the usual sense, if a good cause benefits from a sale, what harm is done? To the extent that the company shares the profit from the promotion with a nonprofit organization, it is a gift.

A San Francisco group (Working Assets Funding Service) has introduced a new dimension in cause-related marketing. In a linkage arrangement, it recruits subscribers to a long-distance telephone service and two credit card companies, undertaking to put into a "donations pool" 1 percent of all charges the subscribers incur. The pool, which in 1989 came to over $300,000, is then divided among some thirty-two nationally recognized nonprofit organizations. In effect, it runs a "mutual charitable fund" linking three groups: the companies promoting the services, the subscribers, and the nonprofit beneficiaries.

Gurin (1989) has suggested the following criteria to guide nonprofits in any offer from business for financial support, and particularly for cause-related marketing:

1. Does the offer qualify as a tax-deductible contribution? If so, it is obviously acceptable.

2. Is it a no-strings-attached offer of outright support from a corporation's budget for marketing, advertising, or public relations? If so, it's again acceptable.

3. Does the arrangement make a profit for the corporation? If it does, it represents not a contribution but a share of the profits from a business transaction. (*Note:* This is the critical issue. Presumably it is acceptable for a nonprofit organization to receive such a share in the profits, even though it is not a contribution, *as long as the other conditions are met.*)

4. Could the offer weaken or debase a voluntary organization's

case for public approval and philanthropic support—the organization's greatest resource for its own continuing financial
help? If so, it is unacceptable.

5. Could the offer blur the public's understanding of the differ-
    ence between philanthropy and business? That distinction is
    essential if philanthropic support of voluntary organizations is
    to continue.

6. Could the offer enhance the image and increase the sales of a
    company providing a product or service considered harmful to
    the public? If so, there is an ethical basis for declining the offer.

Still another consideration: A nonprofit organization should
not become overly dependent on a company's current marketing
strategy, which is subject to abrupt and arbitrary change.

The choice of whether to proceed with a cause-related marketing arrangement, if it is offered or available, clearly rests with the
nonprofit organization. Boards are well advised to be involved in
the decision.

31. Professionalism, Ethics, and Regulation

When development officers and fund-raising consultants—those en-
gaged full time in fund-raising activities—hold themselves to be
professional, they run into the difficulty of defining the term *professional*. They see themselves in a vocation requiring advanced
training and mental rather than manual work, and they are guided
by two important norms: They approach their assignments and
responsibilities in an organized manner based on accepted practices
and experience tested over time, and they strive to achieve full public acceptance of the professional character of their occupation.

A recently published study entitled *Fund Raising as a Profession*, by the Clearing House for Research on Fund Raising of the
University of Maryland, after outlining the steps an occupation
takes in the professionalization process and the several attributes
usually found with well-established professions, concludes realisti-
cally: "[F]und raising is not yet a profession. At least, it is not
among those few occupations that society generally recognizes as
true professions." The report goes on to say: "Evidence exists . . .

supporting the contention that *fund raising is an emerging profession*—an occupation that has moved steadily along the professional continuum; an occupation with the potential to attain greater professional stature" (Carbone, 1989, p. 46).

Although this matter of professionalism is not a central concern to board members, they have an interest and often ask questions about it. They should be sensitive to three matters: the *organizations* that play leading roles in establishing regulatory mechanisms and standards of practice, *systematic knowledge and a set of skills,* and *ethics.*

In addition, boards have an interest in the related matter of government *regulation* of fund-raising practices.

Professional Organizations

Fund-raising practitioners, including both development officers of nonprofit organizations and independent fund-raising consultants, have four principal organizations: National Society of Fund-Raising Executives (NSFRE), American Association of Fund-Raising Counsel (AAFRC), National Association of Hospital Development (NAHD), and Council for Advancement and Support of Education (CASE). In addition, special organizations have been formed for planned giving and for prospect researchers (those who assist organizations in looking for prospective donors).

The principal organizations cooperate but have not developed a common set of agreed-on principles and standards of practice to cover all members. NSFRE has a procedure by which, with an examination and a review of career experience, fund-raising practitioners can receive a certificate—Certified Fund Raising Executive (CFRE). This certification, however, is not fully accepted throughout the profession, much less by others. The mechanics and discipline of self-regulation have yet to be established.

Knowledge and Skills

The Clearinghouse study found: "The importance of theoretical principles to guide fund-raising practice is widely accepted by fund raisers. Happily, there is evidence that this knowledge base is growing. Yet most fund raisers are convinced these principles are best learned on the job rather than through formal preparation programs . . . [which] create a serious impediment to professionalization of the fund-raising field" (Carbone, 1989, p. 44).

Many groups, both for-profit and not-for-profit, offer widely promoted training courses, seminars, and conferences on all aspects of fund raising. A growing number of credit-granting academic programs deal generally with management and administration of nonprofit organizations. Those that do, however, are for the most part either schools of education, specializing in school administration, or schools of business or government administration with limited adjunct courses in nonprofit administration. The implication is that nonprofit management is only an accessory to business or government management. Moreover, in their curricula these programs tend to downplay fund raising, the one aspect upon which the livelihood of nonprofit organizations depends, and which, more than any other, distinguishes nonprofits from business and government.

Ethics

Although the accepted principles of sound management and fiduciary responsibility pertain also to fund raising, trustees must be aware of several ethical issues that apply particularly to fund raising. They are controversial.

Donor's Designations. Donations must be used for the donor's intended purposes. This is a clear-cut rule, but the temptation to stray can be strong.

Fund-Raising Expenses. As was mentioned earlier, organizations should be prepared to disclose full accounting of fund-raising expenses and what portion of donations directly serves the charitable purposes of the organization.

Solicitation by Fund-Raising Consultants. A firm retained to *advise* does not itself directly solicit or collect contributions. A borderline situation arises when a professional planned giving consultant accompanies a representative of the nonprofit organization, even as a financial or legal adviser will accompany the donor, to work out the technical aspects of a gift arrangement.

Although fund-raising firms can be retained to *solicit* and *collect* contributions by mail, telephone, or in person, such arrangements raise questions both of ethics and responsibility. Board members should be alert to both.

On the ethical side, many firms retained to solicit contributions on behalf of a nonprofit organization are altogether straightforward in their activities. Incidents of unscrupulous fund-raising practice do sometimes arise, however, when the fund raising is contracted with an outside firm. Undue pressure in soliciting contributions, unfulfilled promises, irresponsible appeals for the handicapped—practices over which government agencies seek to increase regulatory control—emerge when nonprofit organizations put their fund raising in the hands of others.

From the standpoint of responsibility, turning over the fund raising to outsiders in most cases reflects an effort by an organization and its board to escape a fundamental responsibility. Moreover, it rarely works. Members of the organization and volunteers tend to be far more effective than hired hands; donors see the difference. In effect, contracting your fund raising is putting your reputation in another's hands.

Commission Fund Raising. Professional fund-raising associations like to adhere to an ethical standard that requires members to work for a salary, a retainer, or a set fee, and not for a commission based on the amount of money raised. They believe that commission-based reward, which is in fact a widespread practice, especially with contract fund-raising outfits using door-to-door and telephone solicitations, raises doubts as to whether the solicitations are to benefit the solicitor or the charitable organization, and whether commission selling offers inducements to put excessive pressure on the contributor. Establishing such strict ethical standards, however, presents the possibility of being in restraint of trade and competition.

Another problem arises in this regard: It is often difficult to draw a distinction between an unwanted percentage-based compensation and a legitimate bonus arrangement to reward the strong performance of development personnel.

Finder's Fees. Planned giving specialists in particular have made an effort to eliminate rewards for financial advisers who arrange charitable gifts purely as tax shelters rather than for philanthropic purposes and place the gifts with institutions for a fee. It is viewed as selling charitable donations, a serious distortion of philanthropy; if seen as tax evasion, it will perhaps invite congressional measures that will deter legitimate planned giving donations. The practice is particularly objectionable when such a gift is offered widely and placed with the highest bidder. It is well for an institution to avoid this difficulty by making a practice of dealing directly with the donor.

Conflict of Interest. Board members, employees, and consultants of a nonprofit organization should disclose in writing any interest they or their families have in any business association that seeks to contract with the organization. To avoid conflict of interest, or the appearance of conflict of interest, they should abstain from any action involving that business. Fund-raising counsel and other firms, such as lawyers, investment bankers, and real estate agents, must be particularly scrupulous in avoiding participation when their occupational relationships come into contact with the organization with which they have a fiduciary responsibility or a family relationship.

Conflict of interest leads to a related matter on which there is some difference of view. Not all boards agree that their members drawn from the legal, accounting, fund-raising, and similar fields should not be called upon to do their professional work for the organization. Generally, organizations should retain such legal, accounting, and fund-raising counsel as they require, even if on a *pro bono* or reduced-fee basis. Board members can contribute to policy decision making and oversight of performance in their fields of enterprise, but they should not be asked to contribute what they sell professionally.

Regulation

Just as boards are concerned with professionalism and ethics, so must they be familiar with government regulation.

Numerous new state laws and regulations, differing from state to state, call for registration and licensing, financial reporting on institutional and fund-raising expenses, solicitation disclosures (oral declaration or display of license when asking for a contribution), or liabilities for damages and compensation for wronged donors. Fully enforced, these laws would be excessively restrictive, imposing unreasonably stiff penalties for violations and putting an administrative burden on legitimate fund-raising practices, consultants, and institutions. Although recent court decisions have questioned the constitutionality of these actions, some states, prompted by well-publicized charity scandals and tales of innocents duped by unscrupulous solicitors, are still compounding restrictive regulations.

The AAFRC annually publishes a comprehensive review of all these laws, entitled *Annual Survey: State Laws Regarding Charitable Solicitations.*

As part of their stewardship, boards need to be aware of legal and ethical considerations in fund raising. Someone on your board should keep an eye on these issues.

32. Using Consultants

A distinction was made in Section Thirty-One between fund-raising consultants who advise and those who solicit and collect contributions. Here the discussion is confined to advisory counsel.

Board members confront two questions: *When is outside counsel appropriate?* and, if it is, *How do you find the right counsel* for you?

When to Use Consultants

Fund-raising counsel can advise on how to raise *capital funds,* can make comprehensive *audits* of development programs, and can give *advice* on specific fund-raising problems.

Capital Funds. Chapter Five discussed three ways of raising capital funds: capital campaigns, planned giving, and insurance. On capital campaigns, it stated categorically that only through a *feasibility study* conducted by an outside, professional fund-raising counsel can an objective evaluation be made of (1) the strength of an organization's support constituency on which to base a realistic estimate of the potential and a reasonable goal, and (2) the readiness of the organization to undertake such a major endeavor as a capital campaign. In addition, in a feasibility study counsel will prepare a thorough plan for a campaign: staff and volunteer organization, publicity and printed materials, timeline, costs—all phases of effective planning and execution.

Raising capital funds through planned giving and insurance programs clearly involves technicalities beyond the usual competence of a development staff; outside counsel can lead the way.

Fund-Raising Audits. As was discussed in Section Twenty-Nine, nonprofit organizations have a right to be concerned about the effectiveness of their development programs. Boards may be troubled about their own leadership, staff strength, public relations, and any one of the many components of a fund-raising program. They may question their management of automation, printed materials, and budget planning. They know that the competition for the given dollar is intense; are they equipped to enter or stay in the arena?

To help them, a professional can make an *audit* of their position and the steps available to them for an effective development program. Such a thorough evaluation can assist both board and staff to reach the best courses of action to strengthen their fund-raising efforts.

In the same way that well-run companies regularly retain management consultants to review their operations, nonprofit organizations can call in outside counsel to evaluate their fund-raising performance, confirm activities that are on the right track, and modify others. Professional counsel, having looked at other organizations with similar problems, reviews operations from a wide perspective and identifies the areas that call for priority efforts. An audit presents an overall strategy for moving ahead.

Advice. Boards and chief executives need someone on whom to test their ideas. Fund-raising counsel can serve that function. They can be called on when needed, give advice when asked, and confirm, from their experience, what is being done right. Wise heads have said that consultants call tell boards and executives what nobody else dares to. Boards listen to consultants when they can't hear the same message from the staff.

How to Obtain Counsel

Fund-raising counsel is not hard to find; the problem is to get the right one for the right job. When searching for a consultant for any of the foregoing purposes, board members should assure themselves on three key matters:

1. *Be clear on the consulting job to be done.* Insist on written proposals from applicants. Make sure the proposals include the objective of the task, the manner in which it will be carried out, the contents of the report, the time it will take, and the costs, including expenses.
2. *Be sure who is going to do the job.* You are buying a person, not a company. Interview the one who will carry out the feasibility study or audit and will interview important constituents on your behalf. The representative who sells you the proposition may not be the one to do the job—find the one who is and conduct intensive interrogation.
3. *Check references.* Check all of them, scrupulously. Were previous clients fully satisfied? The principle of *caveat emptor* should prevail.

Not infrequently boards are confronted by the argument that their organization should manage its own fund-raising responsibilities, including raising of capital funds, without expensive outside help. It's a valid stance, but it must be knowledgeably dealt with if the organization is to move forward soundly, with or without advisory counsel. The size and level of experience of the staff must be considered, as well as the size of the funding needs and the complexity of the procedures. The board must evaluate the dimensions of the challenge before calling on counsel.

9

Leadership Revisited: Making the Board Effective

33. Board Composition, Organization, and Motivation

You will hear it said that only two things are needed for successful fund raising: a truly worthwhile mission and leadership that is enthusiastic and willing to participate. Although oversimplified, especially in light of the many elements of a comprehensive fund-raising program in which board members have a part, the saying is essentially true. A fund-raising program is only as good as its leadership. Leadership *is* the board. The chief executive and the development office are critical to successful operation, but the ultimate responsibility for success or failure lies with the board.

Three aspects of board leadership are important to the fulfillment of the fund-raising responsibility: the *composition*—membership and recruitment of members, the *organization,* and the *motivation* and involvement of its members.

Composition

Although you always want a board strong enough to carry all its responsibilities, you *must* have such a board to succeed in fund raising. Both size and membership are important.

For good reason, as was discussed in Chapter One, nonprofit boards of trustees are bigger than business boards of directors. Nonprofit institutions need to enlist many skills, reach a wide spectrum of the community, and get the personal involvement of many members in all board activities including, of course, fund raising.

Organizations that seek to limit their boards "to achieve efficiency," or to maintain a "special program character," are not helping themselves; they may be overlooking their wider responsibilities, including fund raising. For successful fund raising, boards need to have members drawn from the whole community, business and professional leaders, people who are known and who themselves know others close to key funding sources, as well as those deeply involved in the program. Nonprofit institutions, even smaller community organizations, should not be fearful of having boards of thirty or even forty members. They should be concerned if the board remains a small, homogeneous, inward-looking group.

Most community service organizations start out life with program-oriented leadership—small boards composed of people deeply involved with the service programs of the organization. Performing or visual artists make up the board of a cultural organization; professionals and social workers compose a community service board. Only when the organization grows to the point where it must have major funding does it require a community-oriented board in order to survive.

People wise in the ways of nonprofit boards say that the *nominating committee,* the most important of all the board committees, should be chaired by the board's most respected member, the one who can attract community leaders. The prestige level of a nonprofit board does not rise above the level of its most prestigious members. Although the nominating committee has recruiting responsibility, every board member, especially those on the development committee, and the development office itself should be ever alert to suggest names of candidates who can bring strength to the board.

When recruiting members, be open and clear about fundraising responsibilities. Although you don't have to put fund raising above other issues, you should be candid: Board members are expected to contribute what they reasonably can and to participate where they can be helpful in ensuring that adequate resources are obtained. It is easy to dodge this aspect when seeking to attract desirable members, and not mention fund raising. (Orientation of new members should also include presentations of the development program and board member participation in it.)

Some board recruiting devices, however, are not helpful. Aggressive leaders sometimes advocate a board membership policy of "give, get, or get off," which is to say that a member, to stay on the board, must make a major contribution (sometimes a stated figure) or be responsible for raising that specified amount from others. This simplistic approach, overemphasizing a member's financial contribution, can scare off good candidates and surely it fails to recognize the complexity of the board member role in fund raising. It overlooks the many skills involved in the activity and excludes from the board many who could strengthen the organization.

Organization

Both board and staff must be active in fund raising. Chapter One noted that every organization must be deliberate in the division of labor between the chief executive, who is usually supported by a development staff, and the board. Be clear, for example, on personal strengths and weaknesses when allocating responsibilities and duties. Some executives are experienced and talented in raising money; others shy away from it. Boards, ultimately responsible for success, must adapt their own activities to support, oversee, or take leadership as active participants.

A *development committee* can help concentrate the attention of board and staff on important aspects of fund raising, bring focus and force to board efforts, and work with and oversee staff. However, board members should never be seduced into believing they can turn over the fund-raising task to the development committee, any more than they can turn it over to staff or an outside agency.

By the nature of fund-raising activities, development committees tend to operate differently from other committees: Development committee members get directly involved in fund-raising activities. Thus an effective development committee

- Oversees the preparation of a comprehensive development plan and strategy (Section Twenty-Six) for annual review by the board
- Ensures, through the development plan, that a realistic appraisal is made of the potential for getting support, that reasonable fund-raising goals are set, and that adequate budgetary support is given to the fund-raising effort
- Participates actively in the selection of prospects, the preparation for solicitations, cultivation, and actual asking
- Concentrates the attention of other members and staff on fund raising and enlists other board members for specific fund-raising tasks
- Calls on every board member to contribute to the best of his or her ability.

Some cautions need to be introduced about board organization beyond that of the development committee. Although the reasons are not related to fund raising only, boards must guard against a dominant and preemptive executive committee. The more an executive committee meets and makes the decisions, the weaker the full board will become and the less effective will be each other committee on which the board needs to rely. Executive committees, while appearing to be efficient, can thus be the scourge of board performance, reducing the effectiveness of even the development committee that it counts on for fund-raising leadership.

Beware, too, mixing fund raising with financial and investment responsibilities. Raising money is different from handling money. Don't expect the finance committee to handle the fund raising, or even to tell the development committee how much should be raised. Similarly, neither the development committee nor the finance committee should be charged with investment responsibilities. Budgeting, accounting, investing, spending, and fund raising are each separate functions. The members of these committees must talk to each other but no one committee should do the others' job.

Another caution: Boards have a tendency to be naive about the time factor in fund raising. Boards must not let cash flow pressures influence fund-raising decisions, especially when finances are tight. Because an organization has to meet a payroll or other commitments by a stated time does not mean the fund-raising program can be adjusted to meet that need. Fund raising has its own time constraints: The gestation period for government, foundation, and business grants can be six to eighteen months; annual giving receipts tend to concentrate at year-end. Though seasonal needs are pressing, they are not favorable guides to fund raising and should not be permitted to influence plans.

A strong board can expect to have a strong development committee but will fully understand that that committee does not relieve the board of its responsibility for fund-raising effectiveness.

Motivation

You can have a sound board membership and organization, but if you don't have board member involvement and participation, your fund raising will suffer. The key is motivation. How do you motivate board members to get involved in fund raising? You do it from above and from below.

John Gardner, in a widely acclaimed series of papers on leadership sponsored by INDEPENDENT SECTOR, says: "More than any other attribute, this [capacity to motivate] is close to the heart of the popular conception of leadership—the capacity to move people to action, to communicate persuasively, to strengthen the confidence of followers" (1987, p. 15). A lively, committed board chair will stimulate and invigorate the whole board in all its responsibilities, including fund raising. An active chair of the development committee will see that fellow board members participate.

Although the chair leadership is the most telling, the chief executive and development staff can do much to stimulate involvement and enthusiasm. The starting point is to make sure that board members fully realize all the things they can do significantly to assist in the fund-raising effort without having to ask for money. Meet the "I'll do anything but . . ." syndrome head on. Show them where they can help from inside. Lead them down the many paths of planning and preparation, of building the support constituencies, of evaluating prospects, and of writing letters. The more board members are involved in planning and cultivating events, for example, the more likely they are to participate in direct fund-raising activities. (Also, the more likely they are to give generously.)

Remember this: *The way to motivate board members is to work with each one individually.* Simple as that advice is, it is remarkable how seldom it is accepted and followed. When you ask each member individually for help on limited but specific tasks, your chances of getting a positive response are good. Conversely, general appeals and pleas at board meetings or through the mail, no matter how evangelical and insistent, will invariably get limited response.

Here is an illustration. Take to a business executive board member a list of twenty companies with a profile of their top officials; ask which ones he knows and how he can help in reaching them. You will get a positive response. Ask the same thing of members in a general appeal at a meeting and you will get minimal results. Similarly, visit a civic leader board member with a list of local philanthropists and invite comments on how to reach them and you will get answers. Little help will come from a general appeal for such information.

Development officers should know precisely what help they want from each board member (some of whom can be more useful than others), prepare thoroughly, and appeal individually. A strong development staff officer, with the endorsement of the chief executive, can be in direct touch with individual board members and should be welcome at board meetings.

The discussion of cultivation (Section Twenty-One) suggested that board members can be active in writing or telephoning to thank supporters for their contributions. Such simple but direct involvement can have an important side effect: Board members will be motivated to give themselves more generously and to participate in other aspects of the fund-raising effort.

Each board member must find what part he or she can play. Development staff must accept this procedure, be patient, and slowly help reluctant members to find their roles. Let members start by doing what they enjoy most and are good at: evaluating prospects, drafting letters, hosting or managing events. Thus nurtured and led, board members come to accept broader responsibility for participating in fund-raising activities and to overcome their understandable resistance.

34. Ensuring Board Effectiveness

Listen to some concerns, even complaints, heard from board members, chief executives, and development officers: "What do you do if you have a do-nothing board?" "Our board does not accept its fund-raising responsibility." "Our board hasn't changed its membership in years." "Our board doesn't have any wealthy members, or anybody who knows wealthy people." What *do* you do?

Some things to do are fairly obvious. As a trustee you seek to change the board leadership, the chair, even when that person may be a fine fellow and your friend. It is never easy, it cannot be done precipitously, but it may be necessary. You look to the nominating committee and the recruitment of new members. Again, it takes time to reconstitute and reinvigorate board membership. You make sure the by-laws call for rotational memberships: A member serves for a limited time and leaves, returning only after a year off.

Other things to do are less obvious. Make sure that board responsibilities, including participation in fund-raising activities, are clearly understood by those being recruited for the board and that a thorough orientation is given new members. Encourage board members to attend learning conferences. Invite a professional to talk to the board; members may listen to an outsider.

If it is accepted, as indeed it must be, that the effectiveness of any nonprofit organization depends on its leadership, on the performance of its board, then it follows that the board has an obligation to evaluate its own performance. It must review its membership, organization, and procedures; it must test its own effectiveness, including that in fund raising.

But board self-evaluations are known to be difficult. Boards are too busy, too pressed in the limited time of meetings, to engage in a serious process of self-evaluation. All evaluations—of programs, people, groups—are sensitive and awkward: They deal with personalities; they subject friends and peers to criticism. Board members see themselves as volunteers who shouldn't be subjected to evaluation ordeals.

One procedure has proven successful. Boards can establish a standing *committee on governance,* a "committee on trustees," charged with keeping the board's own effectiveness under constant review, including, of course, its fund-raising responsibilities.

Such a committee on governance takes over the role of the nominating committee of recommending board candidates and officers, but in addition it considers such important matters as by-laws; conflicts of interest; committee structure and membership; board procedures, meeting schedules, agenda, and papers; relationships of the board to management (the executive); and board member participation in fund raising. Needless to say, the chair of the committee on governance, like that of the nominating committee that it replaces, should be a member of the board who commands the respect of all concerned.

Peter Drucker, in an article entitled "What Business Can Learn from Nonprofits" (1989, p. 91), says, "The key to making a board effective is to organize its work, not talk about its function."

In evaluating board member participation in fund raising, the committee may find the fund-raising checklist (Exhibit 6) a helpful tool and a stimulant of membership participation.

Board members can be slow to accept fund raising as an essential element of board responsibility for leadership. They can be even slower to understand all the activities involved in that fund-raising responsibility. And they can be reluctant to acknowledge that these activities are not all unpleasant.

When board members come to realize the part each must play in the effort to attract resources to sustain the program, they are on the way to making a truly important contribution to the success of their nonprofit organization.

Exhibit 6. A Board Member's Fund-Raising Checklist.

1.	Do I have a clear picture of the mission, the priorities, and the funding needs of the institution?	_____
2.	Do I really understand and endorse the case, why some-one should support my organization?	_____
3.	Do I myself contribute to the fullest measure within my means?	_____
4.	Do I continually offer additions to the mailing list?	_____
5.	Do I assist staff in identifying and evaluating prospects—individuals, corporations, foundations?	_____
6.	Do I share in cultivation of key prospects?	_____
7.	Do I make introductions for others to make solicitation visits?	_____
8.	Do I accompany others in solicitation visits?	_____
9.	Do I write follow-up and acknowledgment letters?	_____
10.	Do I write personal notes on annual appeal letters?	_____
11.	Am I prepared to make a solicitation myself?	_____
	and	
12.	Do I do what I say I will do?	_____

References

AAFRC Trust for Philanthropy. *Giving USA, 1989.* New York: AAFRC Trust for Philanthropy, 1989.

AAFRC Trust for Philanthropy. *Giving USA, 1990.* New York: AAFRC Trust for Philanthropy, 1990.

Carbone, R. F. *Fund Raising as a Profession.* College Park: Clearing House for Research on Fund Raising, University of Maryland, 1989.

Conrad, W. R. *The Myth of Business as a Role Model for Nonprofits.* Downers Grove, Ill.: Center for Creative Management, July 18, 1986.

Department of Public Administration, Baruch College. Report of the "Funding Fund Raising" Research Project. New York: Baruch College, The City University of New York. Printed in *Philanthropic Monthly,* June 1989.

Drucker, P. F. "What Business Can Learn from Nonprofits." *Harvard Business Review,* July/Aug. 1989.

Foundation Grants Index. New York: The Foundation Center, 1989.

Gardner, J. W. "Attributes and Context." Leadership Papers No. 6. Washington, D.C.: INDEPENDENT SECTOR, April 1987.

Greenfield, J. M. "Fund-Raising Costs and Credibility: What the Public Needs to Know." Report of the National Society for Fund-Raising Executives Committee on Public Education on the Cost of Fund Raising. *NSFRE Journal,* Fall 1988.

Gurin, M. J. "Phoney Philanthropy." *Foundation News,* Council on Foundations, May/June 1989.

Pocock, J. W. *Fund-Raising Leadership: A Guide for College and University Boards.* Washington, D.C.: Association of Governing Boards of Universities and Colleges, 1989.

Seltzer, M., and Cunningham, M. "General Support vs. Project Support: A 75-Year-Old Debate Revisited." Paper delivered at the Ford Foundation Donors' Forum of Chicago, June 1989.

Index